Sigbjørn Obstfelder

Twayne's World Authors Series

Leif Sjöberg, Editor of Norwegian Literature
State University of New York at Stony Brook

TWAS 649

SIGBJØRN OBSTFELDER
(1866-1900)
Lithograph by Edvard Munch

Sigbjørn Obstfelder

By Mary Kay Norseng

University of California,
Los Angeles

Twayne Publishers · Boston

Sigbjørn Obstfelder

Mary Kay Norseng

Copyright© 1982 by G.K. Hall & Company
Published by Twayne Publishers
A Division of G. K. Hall & Company
70 Lincoln Street
Boston, Massachusetts 02111

Book Production by Marne B. Sultz
Book Design by Barbara Anderson

Printed on permanent/durable acid-free
paper and bound in The United States of
America.

Library of Congress Cataloging in Publication Data

Norseng, Mary Kay.
Sigbjørn Obstfelder.

(Twayne's world authors series; TWAS 649. Norway)
Bibliography: p. 156
Includes index.
1. Obstfelder, Sigbjørn, 1866-1900—Criticism and
interpretation. I. Title. II. Series: Twayne's world
authors series; TWAS 649. III. Series: Twayne's
world authors series. Norway.
PT8921.02Z79   839.8′216   81-7005
ISBN 0-8057-6492-5   AACR2

189763

Contents

About the Author

Professor Norseng received her M.A. degree in 1966 and her Ph.D. in 1975 in Scandinavian Studies from the Scandinavian Department at the University of Wisconsin, Madison. She is currently Associate Professor and head of the Scandinavian Section of Germanic Languages at the University of California, Los Angeles. Prior to joining the faculty at UCLA in 1973 she taught in the Scandinavian Division of Germanic Language and Literature at the University of Chicago (1967-68) and in the School of European Studies at the University of East Anglia, Norwich, England (1968-69).

She has written several articles on Norwegian and Danish literature of the nineteenth and twentieth centuries, including "Clemens Petersen in America," *Scandinavian Studies* 48, no. 4 (Autumn 1976); "A Case of Mistaken Identity," *Danske Studier* (February 1978); "Obstfelder's Prose Poem in General and in Particular," *Scandinavian Studies* 50, no. 2 (Spring 1978); "Hamsun's Weary Wanderer: From an American Point of View," *Edda* 3 (Autumn 1979).

Preface

Although he wrote for only ten years, Sigbjørn Obstfelder became Norway's major poet of the 1890s and the most important precursor of Modernism in Scandinavia. His works were the blue flower of the Norwegian *fin de siècle,* winning renown in the Nordic countries as well as in Europe. Among Norwegian poets, only Obstfelder and more recently Rolf Jacobsen (b. 1907) have achieved such wide recognition.

Unlike Jacobsen, however, Obstfelder has not been read and appreciated by American audiences. This book aims to acquaint English-speaking readers with Sigbjørn Obstfelder, primarily through original translations and critical commentary on the works themselves, few of which have previously appeared in English.[1] I have concentrated in my critical commentary upon close textual analysis. I believe that both Obstfelder and his potential audience are best served by this approach. I have also utilized previous critical writings on Obstfelder and the period to provide a broader, richer context in which to view his work. I am particularly indebted to the Norwegian critic Arne Hannevik, whose book on Obstfelder has made my own so much easier.

I focus primarily on Obstfelder's major works: the influential volume of poetry published in his lifetime, *Digte* [Poems, 1893]; the short stories "Liv" (1894) and "Sletten" [The Plain, 1895]; *Korset* [The Cross, 1896], a novella which is his most popular work; several Symbolist plays; and the diary novel *En prests dagbog* [A Cleric's Journal, 1900]. Obstfelder's collected works comprise three volumes of *Samlede skrifter* (1950), edited by Solveig Tunold.[2] The unpublished material (which would, if published, fill at least another seven volumes), is in the Obstfelder archives at University Library in Oslo, but is of interest mainly to Obstfelder scholars as much of it constitutes unfinished or duplicative material.[3]

I would like to express my gratitude to the Research Committee of the University of California, Los Angeles, for a grant allowing me to spend time in the Obstfelder archives, and to the librarians at University Library, particularly Solveig Tunold, for the kindness they showed me. I would also like to thank Niels Ingwersen and Ross Shideler, whose encouragement and criticism were most valuable.

Mary Kay Norseng

University of California, Los Angeles

Chronology

1866   Sigbjørn Obstfelder born November 21 in Stavanger.

1880   Mother died.

1884   Graduated from high school.

1886   Began the study of philology at the University of Christiania.

1887   Made publishing debut with article in the feminist journal *New Lands*.

1888   Entered Christiania Technical College as an advanced student to take up the study of engineering.

1890   Spring, wrote a flourish of poems and failed to take his engineering exam; late summer, traveled to Milwaukee, Wisconsin, to join his brother and to find work as an engineer.

1891   Returned to Norway in late summer and had a serious mental breakdown. Underwent psychiatric treatment and was released in November.

1892   Began to write again. First poems published. In the fall traveled in France and Belgium with Jens Thiis, experienced a renewal of inspiration, and became a writer by profession.

1893   Published *Poems*. (Lived in Christiania, Støren, Copenhagen.)

1894   Published "Liv" and several articles defending the writers of Realism/Naturalism against attacks of immorality. (Lived in Copenhagen, Christiania, Elverum, Stockholm.)

1895   Published *Two Novelettes*. (Lived in Stockholm, Copenhagen, Berlin, Paris, Christiania.)

1896   Published *The Cross*. (Lived in Christiania, Paris, Copenhagen.)

1897   Published *The Red Drops*. (Lived in Christiania, Copenhagen, Holland, London, Denmark, several places in Germany.)

1898   Married Ingeborg Weeke on June 5 in Copenhagen. (Lived in Copenhagen, Vejle, Christiania, Paris.)

1899   Submitted *In Spring* to the National Theater in Christiania and published *Esther*. (Lived in Paris, Copenhagen, Augevatn, Fevig, Stavanger, Berlin, Meiningen.)

1900   Returned to Randers in Denmark from Germany. Worked on a long-term project, *A Cleric's Journal,* and began a new play, *The Last King*. Died July 29 at the age of thirty-three.

Chapter One

Background

The Myth

Sigbjørn Obstfelder looked at the world and saw it staring back at him with strange eyes. They are everywhere in his writings. Sometimes they are magical, like the hepatica bouquets that beam at him in February from the face of a child, or the thousands of eyes of his lover's arm, shining as her soul. More often they are ominous. Gas lights peer at him in the night like huge, yellow pupils, and a warm, dark-blue eye meets his gaze in the mirror. God's eye, he fears, lives independently inside him, and a blind woman nearly suffocates him with her caressing, blinding hands.[1]

The eyes of Obstfelder's works betray him. He was a haunted man, painfully self-conscious, never really at home anywhere, and seldom at peace with himself. He was also a very gifted writer with a vision as unique as it was contemporary and the daring to commit it to paper. The combination made him Norway's poet "par excellence" of the *fin de siècle,* one of the significant precursors of Scandinavian Modernism, and—all labels aside—a remarkable, often eccentric writer then and now.

Obstfelder was born in Stavanger, Norway on November 21, 1866, and he died a little less than thirty-four years later on July 29, 1900. Although he began writing as a teenager, his major works are confined to the 1890s, and, relatively speaking, they are few: a collection of poems in verse and a collection of prose poems, two short stories, a novella, three plays, a novel, and several essays and articles. A perfectionist, he wrote and rewrote, never satisfied, never finished. The works he published in his lifetime seemed mysterious to many and were often misunderstood or not understood at all. Yet even as he lived he became legend, particularly to his fellow artists.

To them he was the manchild, both terrified and in awe of existence. Sensitive and life-shy, he seemed barely able to protect

himself from wind and weather, light and dark. Edvard Munch
(1863–1944) did a lithograph (1896) and an etching (1897) of him.
In both the eyes dominate, two huge pools staring out from the
darkness. Swedish writer Hjalmar Söderberg (1869–1941) portrayed
him in his short story "Aprilviolerna" [The April Violets, 1922] as
the little Norwegian poet with no overcoat to protect him from the
cold winds of spring, and the sculptor Gustav Vigeland (1869–1943)
sketched him also as if bowed by the same winds.[2] In a contemporary
painting of Ellen Key (1849–1926)—Swedish writer and feminist—
and her circle of literary friends, Obstfelder is the unrecognizable
figure far in the back shadows, shading his eyes from the light of the
room.[3] Söderberg, one of the friends, remembered him as always
sitting that way,

. . . as far in the background as possible, with his hand over his eyes, shading
them against the light. I remember him one time among many, when he
came into a brightly lit room. "There are so many lights here!" he said
terrified and immediately went to the darkest corner; there he sat with his
hand over his eyes. "What are you thinking about, Obstfelder?" asked
Heidenstam. And Obstfelder answered, in a low, quiet voice with his hand
over his eyes: "I once thought something about God. But I've forgotten it."[4]

Following his death the Norwegian dramatist Gunnar Heiberg (1857–
1929) wrote that he ". . . walked so quietly in life. One can't hear
that he is dead."[5] Obstfelder's life and early death are said to have
provided Rilke with his model for *Malte Laurids Brigge*.

His mythical reputation was at the time based as much, if not more,
on the person he seemed to be than on what he wrote. For various
reasons his works may have been inaccessible to many, but his life
easily lent itself to romantic myth making. He had no permanent home
for most of his adult life, traveling first to America and then from one
large European city to the next. From all accounts he was indeed a
quiet man, not necessarily always preferring isolation but certainly
gravitating toward it. His friends considered him a *noble* human
being, and they did not mean to exaggerate. He was a fine violinist
who for a time thought of becoming a composer. He wrestled with
insanity and supposedly died of tuberculosis. It is not difficult to

understand how the myth of the archetypal, late-Romantic poet grew out of the known facts of his life, particularly when coupled with the reputation of his mysterious works.

The line separating his life from his fictions was very fine. In his poetry, his prose, and his dramas he generally used a protagonist obviously modelled on himself, a sensitive outsider searching for meaning; and he consistently wrote in first person, using the lyrical "I" more associated with poetry until it became one of the most popular voices of prose in the 1890s. Obstfelder was a pioneer of first person narration and certainly paid the price of often being taken for his protagonists. Reidar Ekner (b. 1929), Swedish poet and critic, put the confusion in some perspective, making it clear that he felt Obstfelder was conscious of the danger.

He was surely aware of the risk of being interchanged with the I of his narratives, particularly since his narrator has so much in common with himself, but he still chose the I-form. Not because it was easy for him. . . . He thought that the I-form arose from the urge to dig deeper down; it worked with nuances and made possible catching hold of such things that earlier were unsaid.[6]

Ekner admitted though that Obstfelder did not make it easy for his contemporaries or for us; and thus the fictional wanderer has become hopelessly confused with his author.

Falsification, of course, accompanied myth, leading to a series of factual misconceptions regarding Obstfelder's life. Arne Hannevik (b. 1924), the author of the best book on Obstfelder to date, *Obstfelder og mystikken* [Obstfelder and Mysticism, 1960],[7] painstakingly corrected the many mistakes that have crept in everywhere from the literary histories to the personal records of friends and acquaintances, tracing his travels, dating his works, clearing away false information about him and his associates. Perhaps the most intriguing false assumption was that Obstfelder was physically frail. Hannevik pointed out that aside from his mental breakdown in 1891 and his final illness, he seems to have been in remarkably good physical health, particularly considering his constant travelling, some of it on foot.[8](He is reputed to have walked most of the way from Berlin to Paris in 1895.)

Obstfelder's younger brother, Herman, had earlier characterized him as thick-set with strong muscles, a good swimmer and an avid hiker.[9] Yet his friends and fellow artists remembered him as frail; and in truth their memories may have failed them only in the letter of the law, for Obstfelder gave the impression of a spirit nearly too delicate for real life. In a letter to a good friend, Ada Eckhoff, from 1893 he wrote:

I have been sad. I have surely said it before: It seems as if life rows away from me. . . . I walk in the dark. I pick a white anemone, I hold it in my hand, tear it apart. Why does it exist? And I yearn. From the snow I yearn for the first white flower of the field. But when the first white flower of the field has come with her sisters a new longing springs forth, and I yearn for the trees' dry branches to leaf and bud. And when all the crowns stand fragrant and green, then I look from the green of the trees down toward the earth and ask: —For what am I yearning? For the white, for the white of the chokecherries' bloom. And now the chokecherries' bloom has come too. And always, always I go there guilty and asking: Are you yearning, Sigbjørn, for what are you yearning?[10]

The problem is that the myth has lent itself not only to a muddying of many of the facts of Obstfelder's life but also to superficial generalizations and interpretations of his work. Nevertheless, the myth contains enough real truth to have persisted, as it does even now. Until recently Obstfelder has been a poet for the few, yet most Norwegians could probably quote—more or less accurately—the second to the last line of his best-known poem, "Jeg ser"[I See, 1892]: *Jeg er vist kommet på en feil klode!"* ["I must have come to the wrong planet!"]. The line is very likely the most frequently quoted line not only of Norwegian but of Scandinavian poetry, and the poem itself has become the classic expression of modern alienation. The poet stands in the middle of the city, staring at its facades, looking but "seeing" nothing but surfaces. The sky is strange and the sun bloody, as if it were suffering. A storm is growing, threatening to darken the sky, the city, and the vision of the poet, who seems to have no grasp at all on reality. His vocabulary is minimal and without much meaning. "I see, I see. . ." he repeats monotonously, but he does not really perceive anything. Not even anonymous eyes stare back at him.

The poem admittedly has been used all too often to "sum up" Obstfelder. But the fact remains that although he was much more than the alienated poet of "I See" or the hollow-eyed man of Munch's lithograph, in his writing he was that frightened soul most of all. We must be careful not to misuse the myth. Obstfelder was a deep, varied, and innovative writer deserving of much more than literary stereotyping. But we must also be aware of the truth of the myth. It is the dark thread running through his works; and these works touch us today not so much because of their innovativeness at the time, but because they captured the profound unease of the 1890s which has become the unease of the twentieth century. The ill effects of the industrial age were beginning to be felt in all segments of society. Almost unnoticeably a sense of rootlessness and loss of control was creeping into the lives of many. Of those who had a voice, the artists may have felt the unease most acutely, for they seemed to have no "real" role to play and thus no power in this new age. Obstfelder, as much as any writer of the late nineteenth century, was able to express their sadness, their fears, and their anxieties. He was humble in the face of pain, particularly psychological pain, and thus he could reach his fellows as he can still reach us.

The "Poet" and His Time

As Obstfelder looked first for the white flowers of the fields and when they had come looked impatiently ahead to the chokecherries, he also experimented with different literary forms, looking for the one that could best convey what he personally had to say. He tended to concentrate on one form at a time—although never exclusively—and therefore his literary biography can conveniently and without much distortion be told from the point of view of his experimentation with different genres, first poetry, then the prose poem, then longer fiction, plays, and finally a semi-autobiographical diary novel.

Although he wrote in virtually all genres, he is generally referred to as a poet. This is due in great part to the Obstfelder myth, "poet" being used in a generic sense to mean the archetypal artist of the *fin de siècle*. Similarly, his writings are often referred to as his "poetry." The terms are not wrong, for Obstfelder wrote during a decade when all literary genres were very influenced by poetry. Its lyrical subjectivism was adapted to fiction and to drama and in many cases transformed them both. Obstfelder not only worked with forms much influenced by poetry—and also music—but at least as significantly, he developed a language in prose that is as lyrical as his finest poem.

The lyrical mood of the *fin de siècle* struck the tone for many of the literatures of Europe. The decade was called the "Spiritual Break-through" in Scandinavia and is now referred to in Norwegian literary histories as "The New Romanticism." The decade is most easily, though somewhat incorrectly, understood as a reaction against the problem-oriented Realistic/Naturalistic literature of the 1870s and 1880s, known as the "Modern Breakthrough." These had been good years for Norway, whose national literature was, practically speaking, barely as old as the century.[11] In only two decades Norway had developed an internationally recognized literary life. Henrik Ibsen (1828–1906) was, of course, its most prominent figure; but there were others like Bjørnstjerne Bjørnson (1832–1910), Jonas Lie (1833–1908), and Alexander Kielland (1849–1906), all fine authors in their own right. It was a rich literature concerned with society and the psychology of the individual, and the influence of the one on the other.

But the young writers of the 1890s grew impatient with this literature in love with social problems. In the words of one of the least inhibited and now most famous spokesmen for the *new* literature, Knut Hamsun (1859–1952):

Now what if literature on the whole began to deal a little more with mental states than with engagements and balls and hikes and accidents and such? Then one would, to be sure, have to relinquish creating "types,"—as all have been created before,—"characters"—whom one meets everyday at the fish market. And to that extent one would perhaps lose a part of the public which reads in order to see if the hero and the heroine get each other. But in return . . . we would experience a little of the secret movements which are made unnoticed in the remote places of the soul, the capricious disorder of perception, the delicate life of fantasy held under the magnifying glass, the wanderings of these thoughts and feelings out of the blue; motionless, trackless journeys with the brain and the heart, strange activities of the nerves, the whisperings of the blood, the pleading of the bones, the entire unconscious intellectual life.[12]

Had Hamsun had his way he would have "typed" all the writers of the 1870s and the 1880s as one and the same, found them passé, and been done with them.

When all *is* said and done, however, the crucial difference between the writers of Realism/Naturalism and New Romanticism lay in their definitions of reality; for both believed that literature should mirror "life" but differed as to "life's" core. The writers of the 1890s, of course, focused on Hamsun's "mental states," on the mind and the emotions of the sensitive individual. They tried to reach down to the unconscious, "the inexpressible," as Obstfelder called it, plumbing the depths of the life of the "soul," making much use of moods, fantasies, dreams, and nightmares.

Obstfelder, who embodied this literature of the "soul" for his own and later generations, did not himself feel that it was in opposition to the literature of the 1870s and the 1880s but an organic continuation of it. In 1894 he carried on a public debate in the newspapers with Christen Collin (1857–1926), self-appointed literary censor and protector of the people's morality.[13] Collin accused the writers of Naturalism such as Ibsen, Arne Garborg (1851–1924), and Gunnar Heiberg (1857–1929) of decadence and depravity, arguing that only dirty imaginations could conceive of the moral and social squalor they wrote about in their books. For Obstfelder Collin represented self-righteous, repressive morality—"the moral mob's morality," he called it—versus the honesty of vision and purpose of a whole generation of Norwegian writers. Obstfelder defended the so-called "depraved" literature by insisting on its faithfulness to reality. Life, he said, particularly life in the big cities, "the beating hearts of our times," *was* sick and poor and ugly. The Naturalistic writers needed no particularly depraved imagination but only the eyes with which to see.

Don't say that this is life as it is seen through one of the dark temperaments. Maybe they do find it easier to take notice of the sad aspects of life. But it's certain that it's there, that just behind the magnificent streets where industry shines . . . lie the filthy alleys with their hollow eyes. (III: 257–58)

Ironically, Obstfelder claimed that the darkest vision derived from social reality. Yet as he turned inward to the life of the "soul" he discovered darknesses far more terrible for him than anything external.

In contrast to the Realists/Naturalists, Obstfelder stood for a literature of inexorable subjectivity. He demanded that it, too, be absolutely faithful to life, but its eyes were focused elsewhere, looking for the mysterious realities of the self and the corresponding realities of the cosmos. In describing a fellow writer and kindred spirit, Arne Dybfest (1869–1892), Obstfelder actually spoke of his own literary ideals, finding in Dybfest the essence of the subjective artist. Dybfest had died young, leaving some of the most melancholy and decadent writings of Norwegian literature. Obstfelder wrote:

I have never in any books so instinctively felt and known that I was surrounded by soul, whole and full—not abilities that can do something, not will that wills something,—but soul that must, must express itself before it dies. (III: 279)

He found in Dybfest a vision of the world that matched his own. "It is mankind's spirit, afraid of the dark, yearning toward the light, enveloped by love's mysterious primitive force" (III: 281).

In Norwegian literary histories Obstfelder is generally grouped together with two other writers, Nils Collett Vogt (1864–1937) and Vilhelm Krag (1871–1933), both of considerable importance in the lyrical breakthrough of the 1890s. Vogt came first, publishing a volume of poetry entitled simply *Digte* [Poems, 1887]. Krag received the most positive critical acclaim at the time. Obstfelder, the most original and enduring of the three, was certainly not overlooked. His volume of poetry, also entitled *Digte* (1893), caused quite a commotion. *Dagbladet's* critic called it "the year's biggest literary event,"[14] causing others in turn to call that critic a fool. One critic in particular found the volume offensive, referring to it as "nonsense," "delirium's fantasies," etc.[15] But on the whole the major critics and writers reacted positively to *Poems*, as they did to the rest of his publications. Given the quality and universality of Obstfelder's work, however, he received relatively little commensurate recognition, which had rather serious financial consequences for him as he received very little state support.

After 1892 he was entirely dependent on his writing for his income; and as Hannevik has shown, it did not add up to much.

... he had no other income than that which he got for his articles and literary works. But with the exception of *The Cross* which was printed in three editions, the honoraria were small. Of stipends he got one for 400 crowns in 1894–95 and two portions of the state's travel grant at 1500 crowns in the seasons of 1898–99 and 1899–1900.[16]

His lack of money did not make life easy for him, and he was often forced to borrow at great embarrassment to himself.

If the public did not recognize him as it should, he himself avoided literary circles and schools. Although now thought of as one of the major figures and founders of the New Romantic movement, he was actually in the United States when the circle of poets and followers was forming for real around Obstfelder's good friend, the art historian Jens Thiis (1870–1942), at the fabled home of the Dons sisters in Rosenborggaten 2.[17] One of the more serious groups of poets in Scandinavia formed around Johannes Jørgensen (1866–1956) and his Symbolist periodical, *Taarnet* (The Tower, April 1893 to September 1894). Although Obstfelder spent a good deal of time in Copenhagen, was certainly writing in a Symbolist vein, and published his prose poem "Natten" [Night] in *Taarnet* (February 1894), he did not become an active follower of the group.

He was also an outsider in terms of influences. More than many writers, his inspiration seemed to come from within, making for the uniqueness of his work. For example, in the context of Scandinavia the writers he loved the best were Henrik Wergeland (1808–1845), a Norwegian Romantic poet from the first half of the century, and J. P. Jacobsen (1847–1885), Danish poet, novelist, and botanist from the second half of the century. They were both sensual poets who used lush styles and bold, unusual imagery. Their influences are indeed traceable in Obstfelder's works, particularly in the early poetry; but he soon developed a style quite in contrast to theirs which was simple in the extreme. It is as if he took inspiration from their sensuousness and their daring and then simply went his own way. He was also very taken with Walt Whitman and felt a kindred "blue" spirit in

Baudelaire. We can see Verlaine in his poetry and Maeterlinck in his plays. But in the final analysis Obstfelder's works are personal. That they are at the same time so expressive of the spirit of the age, not only in Norway but in all of Western Europe, indicates how intensely Obstfelder listened to his own life and the life around him.

The European literary tradition with which Obstfelder is most closely allied is, of course, Symbolism, the *personal* nature of his works being the very tie that first binds him to the movement. In *Axel's Castle* (1931) Edmund Wilson wrote:

The assumptions which underlay Symbolism lead us to formulate some such doctrine as the following: Every feeling or sensation we have, every moment of consciousness, is different from any other; and it is, in consequence, impossible to render our sensations as we actually experience them through the conventional and ordinary language of ordinary literature. Each poet has his unique personality; each of his moments has its special tone, its special combination of elements. And it is the poet's task to find, to invent the special language which will alone be capable of expressing his personality and feelings.[18]

In terms of a literary frame of reference, the tendency of this study is to place Obstfelder in a general European/Symbolist context rather than in one that is specifically Norwegian. Needless to say, Symbolism is a large and controversial -ism. Therefore, no claim is made that Obstfelder should be considered a Symbolist in the purest sense. He certainly never thought of himself as one. Neither is any attempt made to debate the numerous interpretations of just what Symbolism was and who did and did not—again in the purest sense—belong to it. But it is assumed that certain literary goals were initially associated with the Symbolist movement and that these goals were shared by many European writers—particularly as late as the 1890s—who wittingly or not followed in the footsteps of the French poets, Baudelaire, Mallarmé, Verlaine, and Rimbaud. A Symbolist work, it seems safe to say, is characterized by a quality of strangeness and mystery, an intent to communicate indirectly through mood and enigmatic symbol, an attempt to imitate music, and a decadent spirit, i.e., a spirit preoccupied with death. Most of Obstfelder's works— with the exception of some of the early poetry—were written in the

Symbolist mode. To illustrate Obstfelder's European Symbolist affilia-
tion the formulations of various critics are used, in particular Anna
Balakian's from her book *The Symbolist Movement: A Critical
Appraisal* (1967) and James Kugel's from *The Techniques of
Strangeness in Symbolist Poetry* (1971). Both critics deal with the
common characteristics of the movement, which in turn provide a
more general context for Obstfelder's own "poetry."

Biographical Sketch

Obstfelder was born in Stavanger on September 21, 1866. He was
the eighth of sixteen children born to Herman Frederik Obstfelder
(1828–1906) and Serina Obstfelder, née Egelandsdal (1836–1880).
He was one of only six children to survive to adulthood.

His early homelife was oppressive. His father, a baker by trade, was
unsuccessful in the market place, providing his family with little
financial support and, from all accounts, with little emotional support
either, being a strict, neurotically pietistic man. In what seems to be a
snatch of a memory from childhood in the prose poem "Isløsning"
[Thawing, 1886], Obstfelder wrote, ". . . it slipped away, it was
partly dark, the glowing darkness of a constricted childhood where the
joy of life was suppressed and whipped bloody, burned to coal so that
all could be black . . ." (II: 243). The family had a history of illness,
insanity, and early death. Not only did nine of his siblings die, but
also his mother when he was fourteen. All these things—the fear of a
threatening male figure, the loss of the mother, the sense of everpresent death, and the fear of insanity—influenced his writing to an
immeasurable degree.

Obstfelder graduated from high school in Stavanger in 1884 and in
1886, after a series of stops and starts, finally decided to study
philology at the university in Christiania (Oslo). Two years later he
gave up the study of languages to become an engineer, intending to
take his degree and then join his brother, Herman, who had emigrated
to the United States in 1888 and had settled in Milwaukee, Wisconsin.
Obstfelder was to have taken his examination at Christiania Technical
School in the spring of 1890 but was prevented from doing so due to
what appears to have been a nervous breakdown. In a letter written in
1892 to the friend who found him that day, Olaf Behrens, he said,

"It was a terrible day—I was mad, or I was afraid of being or becoming mad, or whatever it was. I wrang my hands, tore my hair, etc.—Therefore I had to come back and go really insane. . . ."[19]

Obstfelder's last year at the technical school, 1890, marks the unofficial beginning of his career, as that winter and spring he wrote many of the first poems that would appear in *Poems* (1893), the only volume of poetry to be published in his lifetime. He had, however, been "practicing at" writing for at least six years, experimenting with essays, fictional and biographical sketches, short tales, journal entries, autobiographical bits and pieces, poems, and prose poems. His experimentation with so many forms is itself significant foreshadowing of the later works, but so too is his return, again and again, to the theme of the outsider: a fox, not at all like other foxes, who wants to learn to sing ("Ræven" [The Fox, 1884, III:11-16]); a grotesque little boy who loves nothing but food and whom everyone shuns ("Et menneske ialfald" [A Human Being at Any Rate, III: 9-11]); a very happy little boy alone in nature, hopping over shining stones with flowers in his pockets ("Solglimt" [Sun Twinkle, 1884, III: 6-7]. The moods changed; the protagonists did not.

The first thing Obstfelder published was a curious contribution to a feminist journal, *Nylænde* [New Lands, 1887] in which he spoke fervently for the chastity of men before marriage. It was part of the larger debate going on at the time regarding the morality or immorality of sex outside wedlock. The piece would simply be a curiosity were it not for the fact that it too foreshadowed a dominant theme in Obstfelder's work, i.e., the fear of the erotic woman. In language not unlike that of the later poetry, the twenty-one-year-old Obstfelder wrote: "And when she came near him, that woman's body with its soft, strong, sexual gait, his eyes darkened and he couldn't stand it any longer and he had to run away" (III: 231).

The second thing Obstfelder published might at first seem unusual given the seriousness of his later work. It was "Heimskringlam edidit et emendavit Sigbjørnus, professor literarum et historiarum Sollandarum universitatis Christiani I Roegeviciae," a bit of satire he wrote and published in 1889 while a student at the university. Obstfelder's writings have certainly not perpetuated his satirical bent, although he was a man not without humor and considerable irony. In what appears to be a schizophrenic switch in roles within the context of his adult life, he had written in his high-school days:

Who of my comrades would believe that S. Obstfelder, the always happy one, the coldly ironic one, the easily playful one, but yet the apparently sincere one, sits at home writing outpourings which perhaps are a little too emotional. —Self-study! (III: 81)

Many of his shorter works, particularly some of the poems in prose and verse, exhibit the playfulness he alluded to in the "self-study"; and he did indeed retain his ironic stance, not as a humor-filled writer to be sure, but as a philosophical questioner.

Without ever having taken his engineering exam, but with some very good poetry to his name, Obstfelder joined his brother in Milwaukee in the fall of 1890. Although he was with the one member of his family to whom he truly felt close, his time in America was lonely and depressing. He worked for a while as a draftsman for Wisconsin Iron and Bridge Company. Restless and unhappy, in February he moved to Washington Heights outside of Chicago, where he worked both as a draftsman and as a surveyor. He grew increasingly despondent over his work and his surroundings, involving himself more and more in the study of music which, by the summer, had become a seriously neurotic preoccupation. In May he returned to Milwaukee where he remained until August of 1891.

Obstfelder's mental breakdown had obviously been building for some time. His brother, unaware of the seriousness of Obstfelder's condition that summer, later felt it had started in the spring of 1890.[20] Based on the earlier quoted letter to Olof Behrens, Obstfelder himself seemed to have had a similar opinion. In January 1892, he wrote to his brother, "The illness has presumably had deep and long roots."[21] Whatever its roots, however, his unstable mental condition began to worsen in the spring of 1891 and became increasingly debilitating throughout the summer. No one—with the possible exception of Obstfelder himself—realized how seriously ill he was. After the breakdown he revealed to his brother that he did not tell him what was going on inside him because he was afraid to scare him and himself.[22]

During those summer months Obstfelder kept a journal, here referred to as the "America Journal."[23] It seems to have been intended partially as a private and partially as a literary document, but it is primarily a painful record of the early stages of his mental illness: his growing sense of alienation, his passionate love affair with music, his sensations of being physically oppressed by life, and his experiences of various kinds of schizophrenic hallucinations. The "America Journal" is an invaluable source in Obstfelder criticism. He appears to have used it himself as the model for "A Cleric's Journal."

Obstfelder arrived back in Norway on August 14, 1891. His condition had worsened during the crossing of the Atlantic, and once at "home" he completely collapsed. In a letter to his friend, Jens Thiis, written the following March, he told him he had gone looking for him, did not find him, went to a police station where he "in the cell fought with the angel during the night, the death angel."[24] Later he went naked to the home of a certain Professor Bang and his family. It became a painful memory for him. In November he wrote to Dagny Bang, one of the daughters: "No one in his whole life has been more afraid than I of creating a stir, no one has been shyer, more certain of his own contemptible nature—that it should have such a sad end!"[25] It is difficult not to interpret Obstfelder's actions that day as a gesture of complete surrender.

He was taken to the State Hospital for observation and on August 21, 1891, was admitted to Christiania Community Hospital for the Insane for "psychiatric" treatment. He was under treatment for mental illness until November 2 and was then transferred to a less formal institution, Frogner Colony, for rest and further recovery. He was released just before Christmas and went home to Stavanger, where he remained for several months.

The exact nature of his illness is still uncertain. The medical knowledge at the time was, of course, limited and the diagnosis therefore untrustworthy. The only professional psychiatric diagnosis was written forty-eight years after Obstfelder's death by the Norwegian psychiatrist Olav Kristian Brodwall, in an article published in the literary journal *Edda*. Basing his opinion on the hospital records, Obstfelder's writing from the time of his confinement, one letter in particular to his brother known as the Frogner letter, the "America

Journal," and Obstfelder's literary works, he concluded the illness was most likely to be described as a form of psychotic schizophrenia, possibly catatonia.[26] Obstfelder's mental breakdown, including the visions, imaginings, and hallucinations he experienced during its course, became one of the most important sources of material for his works.

Obstfelder began to write again already in the winter and spring of 1892, working on some poems and the draft of a play entitled *Esther.* But his real poetic breakthrough came in the fall of that year when he met his friend Thiis in Paris and traveled together with him in Belgium. He wrote a number of his best poems on this trip, and afterwards he supported himself exclusively by his writing. He also continued to travel, making his home on the roads and trains and in the large cities of Europe.

A map of his travels looks like a confusion of lines that crisscross and double back upon each other without resolve. His itinerary is hard to follow and even more difficult to remember, but the main literary events of his life and the corresponding places where his works were conceived or completed are as follows.[27] Obstfelder spent the winter, spring, and summer of 1893 in Norway. *Poems* was published in the late fall. He spent that fall and winter (1893–1894) in Copenhagen, where he wrote his first short story, "Liv," and some excellent prose poems. Three of his articles defending the literature of the Naturalists against Collin appeared in the newspaper *Verdens Gang* in March, April, and May. "Liv" was also published in the periodical *Nyt Tidsskrift* that year.

In the fall of 1894 Obstfelder went to Stockholm where he became a part of Ellen Key's circle. During his five months in Sweden he continued to write prose, in particular the beginning of his second short story "Sletten" [The Plain], and most likely the beautiful sketch entitled "Høst" [Autumn]. He continued to work on "The Plain" in Berlin and Paris in the first half of 1895.

He returned to Norway in August of 1895. "Liv" and "The Plain" were published together as *To novelletter* [Two Novelettes]. He began to work on his play *De røde dråber* [The Red Drops,] which he felt would prove to be his finest work. He finished the first draft of the play in the winter of 1895–1896 and also may have been working on the play *Om våren* [In Spring]. He remained in Norway for nine to ten months and then grew restless once again, going first to Paris for several months and from there to Denmark. He wrote the novella *Korset* [The Cross] in Paris and several places in Denmark, and it was published that same year, i.e., the fall of 1896.

He returned to Christiania that fall, remaining there through the winter of 1896–1897. *The Red Drops* was published in 1897. Obstfelder himself began traveling continuously—to Denmark, Holland, England, back to Denmark, then to Germany, Denmark again, Christiania—until finally he went to Copenhagen. There he married Ingeborg Weeke on June 5, 1898. His marriage to the aspiring Danish singer was not, from all accounts, happy.

After their marriage the Obstfelders continued to travel, spending most of the fall and early winter in Paris. His wife then returned to Denmark and Obstfelder followed in the spring. They spent that summer in Norway and in August visited Stavanger. For Obstfelder it was the last time. They then traveled to Berlin where they remained for several months, and then finally returned to Denmark in 1900.

In 1899 Obstfelder submitted *In Spring* to the National Theater in Christiania, and he published *Esther,* the play he had begun in 1892.

When the Obstfelders returned to Denmark in 1900 he spent some time alone in the country working on *A Cleric's Journal* which had been his most serious literary project at least since 1897, and he began a new play entitled *Den sidste konge* [The Last King]. His wife joined him after Easter and they rented a farm for the summer, but shortly thereafter Obstfelder took ill. He died in Copenhagen Community Hospital on July 29, 1900. There seems to be some confusion concerning the cause of death, but the hospital records recorded it as tuberculosis.[28] He was buried on August 1 in Copenhagen. That same day his wife gave birth to their only child, Lili.

Chapter Two

The Early Poetry: 1890–1891

Introduction

Obstfelder began to write serious poetry in the year of 1890. He was twenty-three and not at all sure of himself. ". . . Words, no I can't use words," he commented in a letter to his brother in May.[1] But he could and he was, writing poetry that was both inspired and boldly different from traditional Norwegian verse. These early poems seemed to well up from within and demand to be written. They are for the most part a celebration of life, from the sounds of the rain to the excitement of seduction. In a period of unusual exuberance—particularly through the spring and early summer of 1890—Obstfelder experimented with poetic language and form to find expression for what he called "the inexpressible," the unconscious life still innocent of conventional patterns of feeling and thought. Already in 1884 he had written in the short essay "Allegro Sentimentale":

What are you to do—with all the longings, all the memories—all the great things you catch a glimpse of, all the small things the scrutinizing microscope enlarges? The inexpressible, those feelings which have not taken the form of thought, you want to bring them forth—but oh! the soil is so cold, the climate so harsh. . . . (III: 7)

An experimenter with language, Obstfelder would, nevertheless, always be troubled by the inadequacy of the medium. Even in this year of 1890 he wrote, "Oh, are my words not deadeningly dry," imagining an art that would go beyond language, "an advanced pantomime that could capture the accidental, its bonds and links, the transitions, the play of the positions, the mysterious fluctuations of the lines" ("Børn og kunst" [Children and Art, III: 235].

But in spite of the "word-scepticism" that would persistently plague him, Obstfelder began to write his strange poetry, encouraged undoubtedly by Jens Thiis, the art historian who played a most influential role in establishing both the legitimacy and the beauty of the Neo-Romantic poetry of the 1890s, particularly against Christen Collin's claim of decadence. It was in this informal circle that Obstfelder held his first readings. He perpetuated the memory of Thiis's room, where he found both acceptance and inspiration, in a poem called "Venner" [Friends], written initially in America in 1891: "... the room in sensuous twilight,/ the lamp,—the Indian buddha,—/ Jacobsen's bust in the sun corner,/ the Wagner portrait!" (I:3). The mystery of the 1890s was in this room, in the dusky light, in the spirit of J. P. Jacobsen's poetry and Wagner's music, and in the mysticism of Eastern philosophy. Obstfelder apparently found here the nurturing environment of which he despaired in "Allegro Sentimentale" and for which he would search, literally and figuratively, for the rest of his life.

His inspired mood held into the early summer; but beset by nerves and failing to take his engineering exams, he seemed to have the feeling that a period in his life had come to an end. Joining his brother in the fall in Milwaukee, he wrote poetry only incidentally, intent as he was on establishing himself as an engineer of some sort. Finally he gave it up altogether as the America experience became more oppressive and the onset of his mental illness more imminent. He felt increasingly alienated from reality in general and poetic language in particular. Imagining that he was called to be a composer and to speak through the strings of the violin, he turned desperately to music as the art form that could save him. In the "America Journal" he wrote:

Fru Violina begins to obey me since I have given her my whole soul, she snuggles into me when always before she slipped from me, gently, softly she arranges her strings for me and says, study me, find my weak sides,—then I will be kind to you, then I will make you rich. (III: 140–41)

His obsession with music lasted through the summer.

Music was and would always be important to Obstfelder, though it never again dominated his thoughts so exclusively. As a writer he continually strove to write a poetic language as akin to music as possible, believing such a language could communicate most directly. But what began for Obstfelder in the spring of 1890 as delight in the capability of language to convey "inexpressible" moods through sounds and rhythms ended a little over a year later in alienation from language and a mad flight into what he thought of as the more powerful, purer medium of music.

His deep distrust of language was shared by many poets of the nineteenth and twentieth centuries. Elizabeth Sewell has written of the Symbolists, Valéry and Mallarmé in particular, that "each of them would have preferred, absolutely, either music or silence above the 'impurity' of human language."[2] Yet for them and for Obstfelder it was this very distrust of words that led to a new kind of poetry. And in this initial period of inspiration and experimentation Obstfelder was excited by what language could do, not discouraged by what it could not do.

The Playthings of the Poet: Words, Sounds, and Rhythms

Many Norwegian poets had written about spring, but few had written so unconventionally about it as Obstfelder did in 1890. As late as 1966 the prominent Swedish poet, Gunnar Ekelöf, spoke of the poem "Vår" [Spring, I: 20-21] as a moment of liberation in his own youth.[3] Written while Obstfelder was studying engineering during those last weeks at the technical college, it betrays his desire to be studying something quite different; but more importantly, it delights in new ways of hearing, seeing, and using language.

> To hell with castironpiles!
> To hell with castironpiles!
> Sss . . . such heavenly laxness,
>   bles . . . sed lax . . . ness!
> Red in the green, green in the red,
>   green in the green!
> Abutmentstrengths?
>
> To hell with abutmentstrengths!
> To hell with abutmentstrengths!

> That woman walking over there,
>   has she sorrows?
> She should dress in blue, anemone blue,
>   her hat buttercup!
> Rollerbearings?
>
>   To hell with rollerbearings!
>   To hell with rollerbearings!
> Warmth and . . . barberries and . . . parasols and. . .
>   and butterflies and . . .
> and and and silver in the air and silver on the sea. . .
>   Waiter! Wine!
> Holes in my socks?
>
>   To hell with holes in my socks!
>   To hell with holes in my socks!
> I have sun, I have shade!
>   —the whole world!
> Should just have had . . . a little red-dressed
>   . . . blond darling. . .

"Spring" can quite rightly be called a little poetry revolution in the context of the Norwegian 1890s. First of all, it broke with the traditional uses of end rhyme and strict meter, seeking subtler relationships in rhythm and sound. Not all of Obstfelder's poems are written in free verse, but as the literary historian and critic Rolf Nyboe Nettum has said, ". . . the best of them are. It is this that makes Obstfelder the forerunner of 20th century Scandinavian Modernism."[4] Second, it employs a most "unpoetic" vocabulary and the open-ended structure which would become characteristic of Obstfelder's work.

"Spring" depends upon a certain amount of confusion, or mystery-making, for its effect. Typically for an Obstfelder poem, the "situation" only gradually becomes apparent: the engineering student turned poet should be studying the principles of cast-iron piles and abutment strengths but instead is drinking wine, watching women, and enjoying the feeling of the warm spring day. The poem progresses according to an unstated but recoverable chain of the poet's thought associations until something reminds him of himself—here the lowly holes in his socks—and he ends the poem underlining his lonely condition. In

Obstfelder's later poetry his loneliness is profound. In "Spring," however, the lack of a "blond darling" does not seriously disrupt the playful mood but rather, in its mildly devilish intent, sustains it.

The poem's real devilishness, though, lies in its language. Swear words, technological terms, childlike utterances, pure sounds, and even silences are found equally fitting for poetic usage. But it is primarily the naiveté of the language that conveys the poet's excitement. Like a child he shouts in delight, and as his excitement grows he finds it increasingly difficult to express himself, initially linking together the wonders of spring with the repetitive use of "and," finally so overwhelmed by all he sees that he becomes nearly inarticulate, stuttering "and and and silver in the air and silver on the sea. . . ." In the last stanza he speaks of the sun and shade as if they were toys, the blond red-dressed darling a doll to play with.

Words and sounds, too, are toys for the poet. The technological terms "castironpiles" (*støbejernssøilerne*), "abutmentstrengths" (*vederlagskræfterne*), and "rollerbearings" (*valsekiplagerne*), at the same time as they are rejected as objects of serious study, become marvelous sounds for his poem. He even plays with pure sound, beginning line three with the hissing "s"—suggesting his own agitation—that is sustained throughout. He allows the "s" to become a part of the word cluster, "blessed laxness" (*salig slaphed*), which in the next line he breaks up into 'bles . . . sed lax . . . ness" (*sa . . . lig slap . . . hed*), creating new syllable constellations and nonsense words.

In his use of such defamiliarizing effects, Obstfelder subtly alters our perception, making us read, hear, and see just a little differently. Already in line three—"Sss . . . such heavenly laxness"—he forces us to slow down, to pause in strange places, to listen to strange sounds, and to read as words syllables that normally do not function together, heightening our awareness of the language and its contents. Ordinary things are seen in an unusual context and are thus made more beautiful, more exciting, or simply more real.

The theme of altered or altering perception is also implicit in the structure of the poem. The technological imagery suggests plans for a carefully designed edifice which is, in fact, mirrored in the carefully designed parallel structure of the first three stanzas: lines one and two and six and seven of each stanza have identical metrical patterns; lines three, four, and five are topographically equally long, although the meter is varied, resembling the unstructured rhythms of natural speech; the identical rhythm is restored in the last two lines. But the pattern is interrupted in the last stanza which ends at the *sixth* line with the meter unrestored: "... blond darling...." As the meter is unrestored and the poem in some sense unfinished, so too the structure of the poet's spring world is imperfect. He lacks his blond darling. Perhaps he will find her. Perhaps he will not. The unfinished ending leaves our expectations suspended, our point of view insecure. Such a state of insecurity is, of course, precisely what Obstfelder hoped to induce, the better to alter our awareness, to tear down and reach beyond our set patterns of thought.

Like much of Obstfelder's poetry, "Spring" may at first seem simple, but its apparent naiveté must not deceive us into dismissing it as unsophisticated. Here as elsewhere the ingenuous tone, the freer form, and the open ending are intended to make us see what we have not seen before. As Rolf Nyboe Nettum has written:

... the apparent naiveté is a subtlety that forces the listener to pay close attention. The unconventional form—also characterized by abrupt outbursts and unequal line lengths—is ultimately rooted in Obstfelder's questioning attitude toward life.[5]

Nettum goes on, however, to make the point that Obstfelder's style

is a necessary expression of the spirit of the age, and not the result of accidental experiments. At bottom lies a profound feeling that the old picture of the world is crushed, that the world does not constitute a fixed, well arranged and meaningful structure.[6]

The unfixed world view is cause for excitement in "Spring," but it was also cause, as Nettum suggested, for deep-seated fears and the growing sense of alienation which writers of the 1890s, Obstfelder in particular, sought to express. In much of his poetry, especially that written after his breakdown, he attempted to construct worlds—still landscapes, bare trees, fixed stars, motionless people—but the worlds continually threatened to collapse or to petrify.

Obstfelder lived with the paradox that his relative world view provided him with the surest means of discovering the "inexpressible" while at the same time giving rise to such anguish as to cost him his sanity. The struggle to resolve the paradox is implicit in nearly everything he wrote. His last work, *A Cleric's Journal,* focuses precisely on the human need for things to be in flux—for surely that is life—and the equally human need for things to be fixed—but is that not, he fears, death?

His concerns were seemingly not so serious, however, in the spring and early summer of 1890. In June he wrote one of his simplest, happiest, and best-loved poems, "Regn" [Rain, I:43–44]. If in "Spring" he jostled expectations by avoiding traditional poetic devices, in "Rain" he accomplished the same thing by exploiting them.

> One is one, and two is two—
> hopping on land,
> trickling in sand.
> Zip zop,
> dripping on top.
> tick tock,
> rain this o'clock.
> Rain, rain, rain, rain,
> pouring rain,
> drizzling rain,
> rain, rain, rain, rain,
> delightful and rank
> delightful and dank!
> One is one, and two is two—
> hopping on land,
> trickling in sand.
> Zip zop,
> dripping on top,
> tick tock,
> rain this o'clock.

Written from the somewhat unusual point of view of the rain drops, the poem's intent is clear: as nearly as possible to reproduce in words the natural phenomenon of rain. It is an exercise in rhythm and onomatopoeia, the light, staccato beat and the tapping of the consonantal stops mimicking a gentle, steady shower. The poem, subtitled "Impromptu," resembles a musical score for consonants and vowels, the parallel first and last sections using—in Norwegian—primarily "e," "o," "i," and "a," the middle section "ø," "ei," and "å." End rhyme, assonance, and alliteration also play their parts in producing a harmonious tonal effect. Topography, too, is used to convey the look of the rain, the poem's slim vertical shape resembling its steady fall. Meaning plays the least important role, the experience of the rain being meaning enough.

"Spring" and "Rain" use divergent poetic devices, but to the same end, i.e., to make something familiar seem strange and exciting. Both reveal the pleasure Obstfelder took in the possibilities of language and the freedom he felt in experimenting with words, sounds, silences, pauses, and rhythms.

The Mystical Rhythms

Obstfelder wrote in the "America Journal" that when "lyric poetry was fully developed it would begin to undress and be rhythmical . . ." (III:159). Not only in the poetry of 1890–1891 but also in the poetry and prose of the later years he experimented with rhythm, trying to find the mysterious meters that might capture, in Baudelaire's words, "the lyrical rapids of the soul, the undulation of the dream, the spasmodic leaps of consciousness."[7] But rhythm was far more than an aesthetic device. For Obstfelder it was the key to the essence of life. He envisioned all of life, from the pulsating of the blood through his veins to the racing of the planets through space, as being of one biological organism moving rhythmically in all its parts. But the harmony of life remained a mystery, seldom revealed and little understood. "Rhythm in music," he wrote in the "America Journal," "is the area which is least studied . . . and even less elucidated are the rhythmic phenomena in nature, in the great ocean of air, in the sea, in the storms,—and in human life, breathing, sleep, the circulation of the blood, trembling, fever" (III:155).

Several poems from this early period are best understood in light of Obstfelder's desire to recreate the elemental rhythms. Unlike "Spring" and "Rain," these poems are passionate, often strained attempts to become one with the rhythmic life force. They are not his best poems, but the visions they contain are central to his work.

"Orkan" [Tempest, I:6-7], written sometime that spring, is the poet's frenetic exhortation of a storm, raging with all the power of the earth, the air, and the sea to free his spirit and join it with its own. "Unfold my soul's wide wings!/ My soul embraces the world." He thrusts his arms joyously into the universe and, in the last stanza, dances madly with the storm."Come!/ Let us play!/ Plunge into the ocean!/ Come, whirling leaves!/ Come, ravens, sharks and seas!/ Come, raging clouds!/ We're dancing, we're dancing!/ You and I!" The poem does not build to the delirium of the last stanza but already begins with it. "Gale, storm, tempest!/ Let me bathe naked in your roar!/ Hey, see my white arms!/ My streaming hair, hey!/ Play with my hair, tempest!" The progression in the poem centers on the poet's desperate attempt to merge with the primitive rhythms of the storm.

He shouts in monosyllables and irregular meters, imitating the storm's pounding, violent motion until the last stanza, when the rhythm grows smooth and lilting in harmony with the dance. The same movement occurs in the sounds of the poem which, like "Rain," can be described as a score for consonants and vowels. The liquids, stops, and sibilants are played heavily upon until the last line, "You and I" (*Jeg og I*), when a dissolution takes place into nearly pure vowel sounds. The union of two separate spirits has supposedly taken place, though the poet at the same time retains his identity.

As is so often the case in Obstfelder's writing, the poet interprets the physical universe as feminine, and he responds erotically to it. The storm is a wild, dancing woman in whose presence he is defenseless. He is naked and white; he throws himself down into the grass, his arms outstretched into space in a position of surrender. In effect he exhorts the storm to make violent love to him, to play with his hair, open up his wings, and plunge him into the sea. Through submission to this awesome feminine force the poet seems to grow equal to it and to merge with it in a frenzied dance of life.

In *Obstfelder and Mysticism* Hannevik isolated two central and paradoxical types of mystical experiences in Obstfelder's works. "Tempest," though not a very good poem, is an excellent example of the first type, what Hannevik called "a vitalistic mysticism":

It wells up preferably after periods of angst, and it is ecstatic and born up by strongly erotic visions. Its goal seems to be a kind of merging with the biological development of life and it is associated with the sun, the color red, the earth's fertility, and the mature, erotically aware woman.[8]

Visions of this kind are most common in the early poetry and the later works, in particular the play, *The Red Drops,* and *A Cleric's Journal.* The second type Hannevik defined as

a monistic experience of a calmer, more relaxed and meditative character. It is not as ecstatic and violent. It is usually filled with chilling, cosmic visions and it occurs in connection with the white stars, "the blue," night, and a dreamy, lyrical and passive eroticism. In its purest form it is connected with cold death.[9]

Experiences of this kind are very common in the writing after his breakdown, including the poetry, the prose poems, the fiction, and the plays. These two types often occur simultaneously in the same work, the poet drawn first toward one, then the other; but the two are usually irreconcilable.

Very early in his book, Hannevik emphasized that he differentiated between these experiences, which he characterized as being of a "lower" form, and a true mystical experience in which the "I" of the mystic is totally taken up into the spirit of a superior existence. But he noted—and this is essential—that it is the expectation of the true mystical vision that is central in Obstfelder's work, not the actual occurrence of it.[10] The poetic "I" continually strains toward release, or loss of its self, in the red and blue worlds at the edge of life and death but seldom achieves it. The poet's identity, fragile though it is, is ultimately separate and remains—though minimally at times—intact. A poem like "Tempest" does not succeed because the strain and desperation show through; the mystical union of poet and life-storm is so artificially achieved.[11]

Ironically, of course, Obstfelder attempted to eliminate the boundaries of consciousness, of which he was so painfully aware, through one of the most self-conscious of mediums, language. In this he belonged to generations of modern poets, beginning most clearly with the Symbolists, who acutely experienced their separation from nature and who, in the words of Octavio Paz, looked upon poetry as a way of reconciling their "alienated consciousness" to the world outside.[12]

From the time Obstfelder first began to write, the theme of alienation dominated his works. It is only in this early period that we find so little poetry about the extreme pain of being consciously separate from God, nature, and the human community. But the fact that we do find at this time so much of the ecstatic poetry indicates that Obstfelder's sense of separation was no less acute. Indeed, it was probably greater, given his desperate need to alleviate it.[13]

The urge to break through the boundaries of consciousness takes many forms in Obstfelder's writing: the childlike desire to be like the flowers because they "just take and receive without knowing it" ("Et svar" [An Answer, III:103]); the exhilarating expansion of the self as in "Tempest"; or the profound death wish central to most of the later work. In the prose sketch "Autumn" from 1896 the wise man says:

He who understands dying does not fight against the wise powers he does not know, he receives them, and it is then that life swells strongest and sings sweetest in him. Nature understands better how to enjoy the life of the earth, it understands dying, it *wants* to die! (III: 74)

But the theme of rebirth is also very central, Obstfelder returning to it over and over again, in many different forms, as if he were trying to capture the self as it broke through into another, more harmonious world.

In "Al skabningen sukker" [All Creation Sighs, I:15–18] from 1890,[14] the earth is mysteriously born again out of its own suffering. The poet is not a participant in the drama but more an invisible witness who is finally taken up in the miracle of rebirth at the end of the poem. The drama itself unfolds as if in a strange dream, surreal images of nature's frustration, suffering, and joy giving way to one another without sequential or consequential logic.

The poem consists of three strange scenes which might loosely be described as a statement, a question not directly related to the initial statement, and a final statement which might possibly be understood as an answer. In the first scene nature is anxious and in pain. It trembles with questions and whispers, birds cling together, "reading each other eyes," the flowers don't understand, "and from the west/ row the heavy winds,/ and from the east/ beats the pulse of the sea." Creation breathes heavily, stupidly, frightened, and in pain. Human beings, too, seemed doomed. "Man meets man:/ Who are you?/ Women give birth/ and die." Questions are not answered. Communication does not exist. Life simply reduplicates itself in a dumb process of birth and death.

In the second scene a woman kneels, "where the roads meet," at "the white cross/ veiled/ in 'blood drops.' " The image is of a white cross covered in fuchias, the popular name for which is "Christ's blood drops." She asks the cross, "What is it to love?" She has gone everywhere with her question, even into the depths of the forest to the old wise man; but she has found no answer, and now her foot is sore, her eye tired, and her heart heavy. "White cross,/ why are you crying blood?/ Is love dead?" Only by implication is the woman's question related to the suffering nature of the first scene. Is the absence of love the key to nature's pain?

The scene ends with the woman's question unanswered. But perhaps she has tapped the mystical source. Is not the white cross covered in blood very possibly the "rosicrucian" symbol of rebirth?[15] The poem provides no context whatsoever, leaving the symbol a mystery, but the final scene lends credence to the possibility of this interpretation.

The woman disappears and the scene returns to the creation of part one, with the exception of the men who question and the women who give birth. No human beings are present. As if in defiant reply to the woman's questions, nature suddenly comes alive in steady, agitated rhythms. Things begin to "drip" and "flower" and "mumble" and "murmur" and "foam" and "sprinkle" and "kiss" and "gush" and "blaze" like a magical potion, chanting, as if in answer to the woman, "until now, until now, until now." The rhythms of the poem grow more undulating as the tension increases and the tremendous force of nature is released. In contrast to the paralysis of nature in part one, the wings of the storm come beating from the west and the breath of the sea comes foaming from the east. Finally the image of this pulsating organism becomes a birthing world. "All creation rejoices!/ Because the earth is pregnant!/ and love is coming,/ coming/ in summer,/ in glowing sun,/ coming in pain,/ in world delight."

The same urge to become one with the primitive rhythms of nature so central in "Tempest" is implicit in "All Creation Sighs." The controlling consciousness is admittedly only indirectly a participant in the poem, but in the last verse—told in present tense—it seems to be taken up in the rejoicing of creation. The human beings of parts one and two are absent in the final scene, as if human consciousness, like all individual life, is meant to be subservient to far greater forces.

This poem foreshadows much to come in Obstfelder's poetry: the abrupt shifts in mood, the surreal imagery, the ambiguity, and the imitation of the illogical world of dreams. It is also a poignant example of his fascination with the mystery of birth. It is his "Madonna" poem. In an essay on Edvard Munch from 1896 he wrote of Munch's Madonna: "For me his Madonna is the essence of art. It is the earth's Madonna, the woman, who gives birth in pain" (III: 289).

In the spring of 1891 Obstfelder sent his poem "Venner" [Friends, I:3-5] to Jens Thiis. The poem recreates the magical union of two friends in a vision of spiraling, singing fire. Unlike the naked dancer of "Tempest" and the invisible witness of "All Creation Sighs," the poet looks back on the moment of transcendence, lost now in "oceans and time." He has no hope that such a union might take place again, but he wonders if there is the possibility of such a thing in another world. The poem ends with a question to his friend: "Do *you* think,/ Do *you* think that friends meet on new planets?"

Like "All Creation Sighs," "Friends" is divided into three parts, but its scenes are far removed from "Creation" 's surreal nature. The poet begins humbly. "Just a little tale of you and I," he says, remembering the wonderful room filled with "sensuous twilight,/ the lamp,—the Indian buddha,—/ the Wagner portrait!" Here the two friends sat and "dreamed together of life." In the middle section of the poem the poet vividly recreates the cosmic vision in which the two friends seemed to become one with the universe and with each other.

> Life!
> A sunray hurling itself in unending orbits,

through all things, through all planets,
an unending,—ringing—, firespiral,—
which we cannot see the beginning of,
and not the end of,
and spirit murmurs in,
and sun drips from,
—suns in oceans of light, oceans of thought,—
an unending, —ringing—, firespiral. . .

The vision moves closer and closer to the center of the spiral which is
experienced as first warmth, then God, and finally "Light." The
macrocosmic image of the sun spiral then turns into the microcosmic
image of cells rising and sinking against the light. Perhaps the cells,
too, refer to the cosmos, but it is tempting to think they refer to the
bodies of the two friends which seem to break up and become one
substance: "—there where the one *is,*/ *was* the other,—life cells
floating,/ sinking against the darkness, rising against the light,/ life
cells floating,/ rising,/ sinking." But the vision fades, as does the
memory of the room in "sensuous twilight." The poet is alone in his
"sterile hotel room," separated from his friend by "oceans and time"
and the darkness of the western nights. He seems to be staring into the
dark, straining for a glimpse of the mysterious room.

   In stark contrast to the feminine visions of "Tempest" and "All
Creation Sighs," the rhythmic, spiraling fire is phallic, possibly issuing
from the union of the two male friends. The one is a man of life. He
had "the happier heart, the warmer pulse." The poet himself is a
slightly decadent character, foreshadowing the life-shy, sensitive young
men of the later works, somehow already marked by death. Yet his
friend understood him. "You came to know,/ how I was, yes, how I
was,/ my blood could not surge,/ but the leaves of my soul,/ oh, the
leaves of my soul, they could wither."

   Written in the spring of 1891—just before Obstfelder returned
from Chicago to Milwaukee, where he fell victim to the beginnings of
mental illness—"Friends" gives ominous warning of much of the
poetry to come. It is a poetry taken up with the pain of being separate,
not the joy of being whole and belonging. The fire spiral is always
there somewhere to be remembered, but its memory often makes the
darkness more frightening and reality more difficult to bear. In *A*

Cleric's Journal the cleric experiences it again, hoping to penetrate to its very source, but he cannot hold onto it, as it always fades into the dark.

Her "Many" Faces

There is no more central theme or symbol in Obstfelder's work than women. They appear as children and mothers, as lovers and whores. They are sensual, ephemeral, earthy, and divine. But though they have many faces, they are considered essentially one being. In *The Cross* the sculptor Bredo says:

There are thousands, yes hundreds of thousands of men in the world. But there is only one woman, only a single one. It is the same woman who is in all women, the same slinking phantom,—that can make itself as small as a mouse—and as large and wonderful as a "fata morgana." (II:75)

The poet responds to the phantom woman in classically contradictory ways: as life-threatening when she appears as the mature, erotic woman, the seductress, or the vampire; as life-preserving when she appears as the virgin, the mother, or the madonna. Though such projections were common in the literature of the nineteenth century, particularly in the 1890s, they function in the extreme in Obstfelder's writing. There can be no doubt that he was very troubled in his response to women and to sex; nor can there be any doubt that this deeply affected his poetry. Reidar Ekner has written:

He was a poet who without great exaggeration can be called erotically obsessed, erotic motifs and symbols seem to have forced themselves upon him. . . . With its tottering double morality, the 1890s was an erotically overheated decade. Poets and artists outdid themselves to portray the woman as a sexual creature, and behind the new trends one can glimpse the influence of Baudelaire's demonism, his woman worship and his romantic idea of woman. Obstfelder contributed some to the trend of the times. He dreamed— in oversimplified terms—of the chaste whore. . . . There seems to be, as Brodwall observed, a contradiction between his strong erotic attraction to the opposite sex and his strict demand of chastity. . . .[16]

As Ekner has said, the terms are oversimplified. So too are such categories as virgin, mother, vampire, and whore. But they are valid and even necessary when dealing with a poet like Obstfelder who remained, psychologically speaking, a child in many ways; who consciously used the persona of the child as one of his primary poetic voices; and who saw in the homeless child the perfect symbol of himself.

As frightened as his writing suggests he often was of women, however, Obstfelder was very sensitive to them and in turn to the "woman" in himself. In the prose sketch "Autumn," he says of the wise man:

The cooking lamp sighs, casting a golden sheen over his sharply backward-tilted forehead, an impassive pride rests on his long, narrow face with its pointed beard, but with his first words the pride melts into something womanly tender. It is as if a woman has taken her place inside him and remade him in her image. (III:75)

Obstfelder had a highly developed sense of anima. His poet often feels the woman to be the keeper—if not the substance—of his mysterious soul. He projects a feminine form onto the universe, as in "Tempest" and "All Creation Sighs." He also uses a feminine persona in several of the poems in verse and prose. Among them are two or three of his best poems.

A quartet of poems entitled "Piger" [Girls, I:33–37] from 1890 may serve as an introduction—in the extreme—to the two types of women that dominate his writing. The first two poems are about sweet, young girls, as innocent as the nature in which they play. The second two are about the temptress, sadistic, masochistic, and cruel. In all the poems the voice is the woman's.

The first two poems are sung more than said. In the first the child—a little New-Romantic poet in disguise—sings to herself of the mumbling of the forest and the humming of the river. She seems to hear sounds heard by no one else and be party to dreams perhaps cradled in the woods. She listens with delight to the secret music of nature and to the music of her own heart beat; but as she listens all alone she suddenly hears only the silence of the forest, and her song ends warily as her thoughts drift off: "Prisoner . . . bird . . . / alone . . . sitting . . . / I can't stand it!" The second poem, sung by a girl

rowing a boat, is pure joy conveyed through rhythm and onomato-
poetic sound, capturing the playfulness of the rower in contrast to the
bittersweet mood of the little poet. The poems do not really mean
anything, the meaning lying simply in the fresh, innocent moods of
the girls. Rolf Nyboe Nettum has referred to Obstfelder's technique in
these poems as "psychic impressionism." He wanted, he said, "to
capture the spontaneity and shifting character of the mind of a young
girl."[17]

In the third poem the girl has become a woman, innocence replaced
by a violent eroticism.

> I'll kiss your lips,
> I'll stroke your cheek,
> but your eyes, your eyes—
> I hate them!
>
> I'll cry in your hair,
> I'll lie in your arms,
> But your eyes, your eyes—
> I'll cut them out.
>
> I'll pinch your chin!
> I'll bite your nose!
> But your eyes, your eyes!—
> I'll kneel for them.

This "girl" is a seductress, tempting, teasing, and sadistically
ambivalent to her lover. In a split second she becomes the opposite of
what she was before. Such frightening reversals are less characteristic
of the poetry of 1890 than the later poetry where the woman often
comes to the man as a lover and is transformed into death.

In the last poem the woman proudly sings of the power she shall
have over her lover. Her song is disturbing, even more sadomasochistic
than poem three. "I demand courage of *my* boy!/ But he shall fall
before me./ *My* boy shall crush all./ But I will crush him!" She cries
that she will make her boy/lover a king and wed him with her heart's
blood. But once she has made her lover equal to herself she will then

offer herself completely to him. "I'll give him all, *my* boy,—/ my
body and myself,—/ yes die in hell/ for my king!"

In general in the poems of 1890 the woman is not yet subject to the
extreme schizophrenia of "Girls." In comparison to the later poetry
the poet actually flirts quite courageously with the sexual woman, if
only in his dreams. Nevertheless, the troubling dualism is ever present.

The Fantacized Seduction

The early erotic love poetry is remarkably direct and daring for its
time, and provides a telling picture of Obstfelder's poet/lover.

"Elskovshvisken" [Love Whispers, I:21–24], from March 1890,
is written as a dialogue between two lovers whispering to each other,
each repeating the other's words like two instruments repeating themes
in a musical score. They whisper in rhythms suggestive of their
excitement, the rhythms growing more pulsating as the lovers grow
more passionate.

The woman is the seductress, but the man speaks first. "I should so
like, my tern,/ my sweetest, reddest tern!/ But no—yes no— —."
He is hesitant, she is not. Sensing his fears, she gently invites him to
make love, offering to treat him as kindly as would a mother playing
with her child. I would love to warm you at my breast, she says, hug
you and kiss you, "stroke your cheek,/ heal your mind,/ with mild
names and gentle,/ hum you quietly to dream."

The man is frightened, repeating "stroke your cheek,/ heal your
mind," but not daring to think any further. He can barely speak. "Oh
no— —yes no!" The woman wonders if he is afraid of her songs and
long kisses. He surprises her with his answer. "I'm afraid to sin—."
But he then suddenly seems overwhelmed by her physical beauty:
"—your charming whiteness/ the quiet night, the darkness of your
eye,/ your vaulted bosom/ my blood." The woman replies, "Then
sin!/ Then *take* me!" No longer the playful mother of the first part of
the poem, she whispers that she will link her curved body to his, bind
him with her soft hair, and set his blood on fire with her kisses and
her breasts.

From this point on only the man speaks. As he grows more excited
and afraid his vision becomes more fragmented, and he sees the
woman's face as a vampire's. "Your eye, it binds" and "your teeth—

/ they are white—smiling/ your whispering, chattering teeth!—" He feels his blood flowing in a different rhythm, like the "rocking" of a baby. He asks, ". . . Tell me if I may, may I?" He begins, it seems, to open her blouse in order to see her lovely body: " —this whiteness in here,—/ these cooling wrappings,/ this softness which is woman,/ under life's lining." He asks to see only a "little stripe" of her; but when he looks up he sees a distant face. "You are so silent./ Your lips are trembling."

The poet's wish to "see" the whiteness of the woman is so ambiguously and suggestively written that it can be interpreted literally as the desire to open her blouse or, more daringly, to penetrate her body. The "whiteness" of the woman is perhaps the poet's mental picture of her.

"Love Whispers" is one of the few poems in which the poet and the mature woman enter into a union of any kind. Although love between man and woman is one of the most common metaphors for the loss of the self in another, there is a marked absence of communion in the erotic poems in contrast to the nature poetry. On the contrary, in the love poetry there is often a reassertion of the poet's separateness. Even in "Love Whisperings" the act of love seems only to have begun, and strangely the poet seems lost in himself. His sudden startled awareness of the woman's silent face only serves to emphasize not the union but the distance between the lovers.

The poem derives its tension from the man's ambivalence to the woman. He is seduced but under protest. Preferring to remain a child, he responds to her playful offer to hug and kiss him and hum him to sleep but fears her passion-filled eyes; he thinks of her kisses and the rhythm of his blood in terms of the rocking of a baby; and he uses a simple, child-like language. In another poem from 1890 the poet goes to even greater lengths to protect the child in him from the erotic woman.

"Drikkevise" [Drinking Song, II:26–28] is sung by the poet to his comrades. "Skål" he shouts, "so they can hear us in heaven!/ . . . Everything that hisses and prickles,/ prickles and tickles and scratches and sticks,/ we'll skål for it . . . Hush!" His mood changes abruptly and the scene shifts from the imbibing comrades to a strange, internal image. "Hush!/ Something's climbing inside me./ A large hedge of wild roses inside me,/ shutting in a sleeping virgin./ Who is climbing in my rose hedge?/ Who is picking my roses?"

A chain of erotic images then flashes quickly before him as in a dream. The virgin and the wild rose hedge give way to a musical torchlight parade marching around the hedge, which in turn becomes blue wreaths of women in long dresses. Suddenly they are naked, and suddenly again there is only one woman. "Bodies. Loving./ Ha, see the blond one in the stream./ Her foot. Knee. . . ." But he dares look no further and his fear turns to anger. "Is it you who is stealing my virgin's roses?/ Out! Out with you, whore!"

The temptress driven away, peace is restored in his "garden./ Now there is only one./ One who sleeps. Whom I dare not wake." He describes the beauty of his fantasy virgin in terms equal to his fear of losing her. "Her skin is made of apple blossom leaves,/ Her blood is brewed from the foam of spring evening-wine./ Her nerves are spun of light, of tones,/ her muscles are braided of rosebud marrow." Satan, he says, was thwarted in the design of her body, and God created her soul. He then turns to his comrades and shouts, "Skål!"

Once again the poet protects the child, here the virgin, in himself, shielding his fantasy from disturbing erotic impulses. But he also vents his anger at the woman who dares to tempt him, a whore to be driven away; and he takes refuge in the image of the beautiful child hidden in his breast.

The Softer Portraits

Using a narrator more distant than the frightened lover of "Whisperings" or the carouser of "Drinking Song," Obstfelder wrote a number of beautiful poems about young women, softer portraits than those of the seductresses. These are among the best of the early poems, Obstfelder achieving in them that marvelous sense of mystery—Baudelaire called it "delicious obscurity"[18]—which has become the hallmark of Symbolist poetry in general and certainly of Obstfelder's poetry in particular. The mystery-making involves the careful selection of details and the withholding of information to create a simultaneous impression of sensuousness and obscurity. Obstfelder perfected the technique in the later poetry and the prose poems but already used it very well in 1890.

"Hun stod på bryggen" [She Stood on the Pier, I:46] is a lovely poem conveying the impression of a woman dressed in white rushing to meet the poet on the pier. In comparison to the freer form of many of the other poems, it is highly structured, both metrically—evoking the rhythms of a joyful dance—and in rhyme scheme. The tight form serves to hold the fragile and fleeting memory of the woman in white. Through a few details—the color white, her shifting steps, her blushing neck—the poet recreates the warm, erotic impression she made as she came toward him. First she is seen standing on the pier "in the sunshade's shadow." Possibly she is standing in the shade of the pier, possibly her sun hat is shading her face. The impression remains vague, a silhouette of a woman in sun and shadow. Then the poet sees something "waving white" moving toward him. Is she waving a white handkerchief or is her white dress fluttering in the wind? With each detail the poet gives only enough information to suggest a momentary impression that then shifts as if in the wind. She is nothing but movement as she approaches the poet. "She had hurried!/ She had scurried!/ shifting steps/ toward me." He feels her sweetness and the erotic blush of her neck brush against him. In the last verse his impression of her nearly evaporates into the remembrance of a name stealing toward him on other foreign piers. Obstfelder characterized the lyrical impressionism he strove for in this poem and others like it in his essay on Edvard Munch from 1896.

And what I had seen myself, I found something of in Munch. The color that trembled and lived, shifting every second, the stones to which my eye gave the strangest forms, the girl on the beach whose dress was not a dress but a symphony in white, and whose hair was fluttering gold ribbons. (III: 283)

Another portrait is of the innocent close to death, from the poem entitled "Brudens blege ansigt" [The Bride's Pale Face, I:18–20]. Here fleetingness takes on a deeper meaning.

> The bride's pale face
> I see before the throng—
> the church door standing open,
> the swelling of the psalms.

> Dressed in clothes of white,
> pale as death itself
> she walks into life,
> joy,
> tears.

She is the virgin on the threshold of womanhood and in this moment closest to death. For the poet she is a symbol of spring rushing toward winter, of life continually dying. Her deathlike paleness is like snow on the lily. "Spring comes, spring dies,/ snow falls on the lily's corpse,/ life smiles, life flies/ toward death." The poet finds great beauty and great truth in the symbol of the bride who is pregnant with the seeds of death. "The wreath in her hair must pale,/ the rose at her breast must die,/ the glow of her eye must pale,/ the fire of her blood must die."

The pale bride, or the dying virgin child, was a favorite motif of the artists of the *fin de siècle*. She was written about by the poets and painted by the Preraphaelites and the Expressionists. She was the perfect symbol for an art obsessed by beauty and death, by what Anna Balakian in *The Symbolist Movement* has called "the lyrical sense of doom."[19] Obstfelder wrote little about her in his early poetry, but in all the later works, particularly the short fiction, the poet will seek her out, finding in her refuge and spiritual comfort. She is the real soul mate of the sensitive child/poet, more spirit than body, closer to death than to life, who will dominate the poetry and prose from now on.

The Eye of the Self

> Can the mirror speak?
>
> The mirror can speak.
>
> Looking at you each morning,
>   studying,
> looking at you with its deep, wise eye,
>   —your own!
> welcoming you with its warm, its dark-blue eye:
>   Are you pure?
>   Are you true?

Obstfelder wrote "Kan speilet tale?" [Can the Mirror Speak? I:31] in the late winter/early spring of 1891 while he was in Washington Heights. The surreal eye, staring back at the poet, studying him, questioning him, seems to indicate the beginning of Obstfelder's intense, schizophrenic self-absorption that resulted in his breakdown in the late summer. The probing eye also foreshadows the writing to come, a writing preoccupied with seeing and understanding in a world of shadows. The poetry, plays, and prose are full of these eyes that stare into the self and out into the universe, strained, blind eyes comforted only by tears, eyes literally afraid both of the light and the dark, held defiantly open but longing to be closed.

Obstfelder wrote very few poems during his months in America. "Friends" and "Can the Mirror Speak?" were written there, and several others as well,[20] but poetic language, for the most part, frustrated him, and he turned to music. Words became his nemesis. In the "America Journal" he wrote:

I want to believe again—in beauty. I want to read Jacobsen as I read him then—all of six years ago—in trembling delight—without the deadly comparisons, oh how they have cowed me, made me small and poor, made me petty, pitiful and wordless, made me meaningless and stuttering, taken my courage and my wits and everything—almost my life. (III:134)

The words were killing him. In the late spring of 1891, in the first draft of a poem he was later to rewrite, he said, "Working their way up tonight/ in a sick spirit/ in a nervous man,/ words./ Words./ My life is words./ Words, withering,/ thousands of stiffening heartbeats."[21]

He had, however, written some very fine, unusual, and even revolutionary poetry. He had broken down rigid forms and substituted the mystery and the illogic of dreams. He attempted to use language to get beyond language. And he established the major themes of his later works: the poet as child, his need to see and understand, his love and his fear of women, his profound sense of separateness, and his desperate wish to be taken up into a superior being.

Chapter Three

The Later Poetry

Demonic Rededication

In the summer of 1892 several of Obstfelder's poems, including "She Stood on the Pier" and "Rain," were published in *Samtiden*'s July issue under the title "Rhytmiske stemninger" [Rhythmic Moods].[1] Although pleased finally to have received public recognition, Obstfelder was disturbed by the attention he attracted. He wrote to Jens Thiis: "Reading my name in *Dagbladet*, this long, heavy, ugly, uncommon name, I got hot behind my ears, nauseous. How—why did I get into this? I became nauseous, frightened. It was as if I had committed a crime."[2] This private image of someone frightened of exposure in a hostile world became the public image of Obstfelder's protagonists from 1892 on.

After a period of convalescence in the winter of 1891–1892, he slowly began to write poetry again; but he did not really regain the confidence or the will to devote his energies exclusively to writing until he met Thiis in Paris in the fall and traveled with him in Belgium. From what Thiis has said, Obstfelder at last found peace of mind, and the poems simply came "gushing forth."[3] Obstfelder in turn attributed his "rebirth" to Thiis, saying in a letter to him, "It is very possible that without that trip down to you I would not have begun to write again."[4] The majority of the later poetry was written in 1892–1893. When *Poems* was published in the late fall of 1893 Obstfelder had already begun to work with other literary forms, primarily the prose poem and the short story. While he did not stop writing poetry in verse, he produced relatively little of it throughout the remainder of the 1890s.

The later poetry shares a greater affinity with contemporary European Symbolist poetry than did that of 1890–1891. Hannevik suggested that Thiis had introduced Obstfelder to Verlaine and Baudelaire and possibly Maeterlinck.[5] But even those poems most likely written before the trip to the Continent reflect the common moods and concerns of Symbolism. In her book *The Symbolist Movement*, Anna Balakian observed:

With symbolism, art ceased in truth to be national and assumed the collective premises of Western culture. Its overwhelming concern was the non-temporal, non-sectarian, non-geographic, and non-national problem of the human condition: the confrontation between human mortality and the power of survival through the preservation of the human sensitivities in the art forms.[6]

Obstfelder's poetry is no exception, focusing on Symbolism's favorite themes: beauty, death, alienation, loneliness, and communication.

He also became a finer craftsman, writing poems more unique and at the same time more truly Symbolist, i.e., poems designed to evoke a mood primarily through the multi-meaningful or ambiguous symbol.

Obstfelder interpreted his rededication to poetry as a macabre exchange of his soul for inspiration. In the fall of 1892 he rewrote the poem about the young man dying of withering words, calling it "Ene" [Alone, I:10–13]. "I had fire enough when I was young,/ —fire enough,—." But the fire was extinguished and now words work "their way up tonight/ in a tortured man/ in a haunted soul,/ words." The words are to him like his own stiffening heartbeats. But suddenly he seems to come to life again, conscious of his own heart beat which makes him conscious of God, "you who creates!/ —pain,/ seeds,/ words—." Often in Obstfelder the poet's awareness of his pulsing blood and beating heart precedes a moment of inspiration or mystical vision. In "Alone" just such a moment occurs as the poet is temporarily caught up in the ecstasy of his own sounds and words which seem to be whispering the name of Jesus to him, "you—/ whose human name/ loneliness/ again and again/ whispers round me/ wafts and whispers,/ hums in unknown voices." But the moment ends and the poet is left alone, seemingly identifying with the suffering Christ and asking him if he remembers "—this tortured man,/ who only, only, only/ has words—/ do *you* remember it then?" Rather abruptly, part one of the poem ends here.

In part two the poet is alone as ". . . the spirits of the dark wander/ on tip toe/ into my room." Strange visions emanate from the darkness, female forms and hearts sobbing in the corner, spirits sighing of death and night; and at this moment the poet is reborn, giving himself up to his demonic muse, the Queen of Death, in a defiant, blasphemous gesture against the god who could not help him in part one. He feels himself a marked man; and "the one,/ whom the Death Queen/ has so marked,/ Death Queen, Death Queen,/ he/ is by day alone on earth."

The conception of the poet as one singled out by the demonic muse to be a stranger on earth is, of course, a commonplace in Romantic literature of all ages. Few took it so to heart, however, as did the writers of the 1890s. The Danish poet Johannes Jørgensen (1866–1956) asserted, for example, that Baudelaire was constitutionally incapable of being a part of life because at his birth a wicked fairy had touched his soul with a drop of sap from the Romantics' blue flower. "He is born in the sign of the moon; under its power his soul swells in the flow and disappears in the ebb."[7] A similar stranger, marked by death, paradoxically owing his very life to it, becomes Obstfelder's predominant narrator in both the poetry and prose. Though he does not always speak of it he is nonetheless aware of death's constant presence, whether in the falling leaves or frightened flowers, in the lover's pale skin, or in the icy blue calm that settles over many of the later poems.

Much of the jubilation of 1890 is gone from the poetry, replaced in part by this fascination with death. Obstfelder by no means discounted the earlier poetry, however. It is apparent that when preparing the order of *Poems* he worked with an organizing principle of extreme contrast—radical fluctuations in mood—indirectly making the statement that the real mysteries of life lie in its extremes and its contradictions. The volume begins, for example, with "Friends," the vision of transcendence now lost but perhaps someday to be regained; followed by the later poem, "Eve," in which the terrified poet stares out into an empty universe; followed by "Tempest," the mad, erotic dance with life. "I have done everything," Obstfelder wrote to a friend, "to find the naive expression to convey the movement between two different poles of my soul in its youth."[8] The range in mood in the poetry of 1892 and after is expansive but plays in a darker register than the earlier poetry on wonderment, ennui, angst, alienation, and ominous bliss. Each mood has its opposite, the beautiful exposing the ugly, the leer revealing the smile. Through the contradictions Obstfelder hoped to conjure from life its beauties and its truths.

A *Danse Macabre*

European poetry at the end of the nineteenth century was, as described by Balakian, "a *danse macabre,* in which death, the great and formidable intruder, waits in the shadows, mingles with us, takes his mask off at the least expected moment."[9] Ironically, as Obstfelder was recovering from a period of complete mental and physical isolation, he began to write poetry clearly reflecting the common mood. Those poems thought to be from the winter and early spring months of 1892 all speak of death as this fascinating intruder, bound up with darkness and night and, most often, beautiful women.[10]

"Han sår" [He Sows, I:48] is Obstfelder's *"fleur du mal."* In a meter reminiscent of the medieval Norwegian folk ballad, the narrator sings of the competing powers of life and death.[11] Death is the unquestionable victor.

> And day it goes in laughter and song,
> And death he sows in the night so long.
> Death, he sows.
>
> He goes and sows,
> sows and sows—
> frightened roses, pale tulips,
> black violets and sick hyacinths,
> mimosa.
>
> He goes and sows,
> sows and sows—
> pale smiles, fearful tears,
> black agonies and sick longings,
> doubt.
>
> And day it goes in laughter and song,
> and death he sows in the night so long.
> Death, he sows.

The power of this terrible gardener sowing his sick flowers is ancient and absolute. The ballad meter and bardlike narrator implicitly suggest centuries of time and wisdom, the steady, monotonous repetition of "goes" and "sows" death's irreversible work. The day may naively skip along like a child, laughing and singing, but death will undo it by night.

"He Sows," like most of Obstfelder's better poems, gives the impression of extreme simplicity. Obstfelder seems to have commented on his intentions with this poem—perhaps unwittingly—again in his essay on Munch from 1896.

In the picture *Death* there are only two colors against each other, the death bed's bluish, spring's light green. But it can still grip you like one of those simple folk ballads that announces death but has a refrain about spring. (III: 284)

Hannevik thought the poem too one-sided, Obstfelder dwelling "monomaniacally on death's terrible power over people and nature."[12] Yet using a technique similar to Munch's "two colors against each other"—juxtaposing day and death, less obviously youth and age, the simple form of the ballad poem and the decadent flowers colored in fear and sickness—Obstfelder achieves beauty through contrast, a beauty that slightly relieves the pessimism and relaxes the grip of death.

A far more chilling poem is "Billet Doux" (I:69–70), dated February 1892. Now it is the woman who emerges from the darkness, itself a vampire sucking the heart of the dying poet. His love letter is an invitation to her to come laugh with him in death. "Come dear lady!/ Come if you please!/ Come in darkness,/ oozing cold and wet/ round a dying man/ sucking a dying heart." Nothing relieves the blackness of "Billet Doux." Only in the prose poems do we find the same unrelenting angst projected through a fusion of death, woman, and the night.

In "Har gåt og higet" [Yearning, I:48–49], the woman and death are again inseparable as the poet longs for the woman to come to him in a fantasy of sun and fire. "I've yearned for warm eyes,/ sparkling with life's glow,/ while chestnut locks shade/ sunskin./ I've yearned for kisses, embraces!/ burning with life's glow/ and black eyes kindling/ sunfire!" But when the woman comes to the poet as his bride in the night, she unexpectedly "removes her mask," baring the face of a corpse. "Her life glow was put out,/ her arms, her mouth closed,/ death pale." The poet's fear of the erotic woman, apparent in the earlier "Drinking Song," is fully revealed in this strangely beautiful, very decadent poem.

Regarding the deadly eroticism of "Yearning," Hannevik has written:

In three short verses the poem describes how the purely erotic dream of love . . . suddenly and appallingly can be turned into the darkest despair, even to images of death. Eroticism in its biological context is directly dangerous. It is accompanied by death. It seems as if a psychic mechanism in Obstfelder's mind again is dramatically triggered but here in the opposite direction from the expectancy of pleasure to despair.[13]

Hannevik was referring, in comparison, to the abrupt changes in mood in a poem like "All Creation Sighs," which shifts quickly from alienation to joy. This phenomenon of reversal is central in Obstfelder's work, particularly, but not solely, in connection with erotic themes; and certainly it sprang from his peculiar psychology and pathology. But we must bear in mind that he consciously used the phenomenon as an aesthetic device, as did many of the poets of his time. It was a way of achieving emotional intensity and assuring emotional impact. Often finding truth in extreme juxtaposition, the poets used the device as a way of viewing the world "poetically," of seeing the goddess in the whore, the seeds of death in the bride, the filth behind the beautiful facades of the modern city.

"Kval" [Agony, I:28–30] is a longer poem which is also dark in mood and dependent on the reversal device. The poet's despair, his "—slinking agony—/ poisonous, consumptive agony!" is caused by the erotic woman. He calls her "she—a whore!" "My heart bleeds,—writhes, contracts,/ *She* twists her hips in soft blankets,—."

The poem opens onto a dark landscape of roses, moon, marsh, and trees into which the poet seems to be trying to escape from the memory of the woman; but she is everywhere. "Womensmiles everywhere!/

Womenwhispers, womenhands!'' Her memory, beautiful and repulsive to him, is so powerful that it invades all of nature.

> She is so beautiful—white, soft, warm,—
> her white neck on the white pillow,
> her brown hair swelling, billowing—
> Why are you trembling, lilies?
> She stole her hands round my throat—
> Damn it all, why are you quivering?

He had come to this marsh landscape to find comfort, to cry in the "wet earth," but it trembles under him, perhaps as the woman did, and he cries out in pain as if he were dying.

Suddenly the landscape is transformed into a place of death, the poet sitting alone in the moonlight among dead men, "with a long, trembling shadow/ a freezing man." The feverish nightmare of the marsh gives rise, or gives way, to this vision of death.

But then once again the landscape changes as the poet stares up at the stars, "God's thoughts," as he calls them. The sky, peaceful, pure, and cold, is in absolute contrast to the moonlit marsh which was wet and warm and symbolic of the woman. The heavens liberate the spirit as the marsh entrapped it. The poet perceives the world in terms of the classic divisions of masculine and feminine, sky and earth, flesh and spirit, sin and grace. There is little doubt that he feels he does not belong to earth. Twice he refers to himself as a god, unable to comprehend that the woman would dare tempt him, she who is touched by death, whose "whiteness yellows" as the "magnificent butterflies,/ glitter and die, disappear."

The poet does not, however, rest nor does the poem end with the world so divided. From the peace he has found comes a vision of an ideal love expressed in images of reconciliation between the spheres of warm and cold. The two opposing landscapes of moon and stars disappear as the dawn issues from the struggle between the two. "See, dawn's chaste sheen kisses,/ kisses the church tower." Through the new male and female imagery of the tower (now of the land) and the morning sun (of the sky) union takes place, paradoxically and momentarily. Yet, as the sun will inevitably rise above the steeple, destroying the union, the harmony of the poem is broken by the poet who asks the dawn, "Is there on earth among women *one/* chaste?" The poem ends with the question.

Underlying the shifting moods a dialectic of a more philosophical sort seems to be taking place between the worlds of the body and the soul, the dualism temporarily resolved in the paradoxical image—both sexual and transcendental—of the steeple and the sun. Obstfelder will employ a similar dialectic in *A Cleric's Journal,* where the sun once again has a primary, unifying function. In the *Journal,* in fact, he exploits the reversal device to its limit, creating a nightmare from which he barely escapes, even as an author.

"Agony" is a poem that looks both forward and back. It is similar to poems like "All Creation Sighs" from 1890 in which the scenes change abruptly and illogically as in dreams. But these scenes—the marsh, the cemetery, the heavens studded with cold stars—are more clearly now the landscapes of the poet's solitary soul. They become his familiar haunts. He will hide in them and speak through them.

The Bourgeois Mask

The overwhelming pull in Obstfelder's poetry is away from life into isolation and dreams of death; yet not surprisingly the poetry contains its contradiction. Obstfelder at times exchanged the death mask for one quite bourgeois, befitting the perfectly ordinary citizen with no other wish than a nice little family and a cozy hearth. In the spring of 1892, when he was trying to decide upon various courses his life might take, he spoke of his wish to marry and establish a home, believing that his illness may have been due in part to the fact that he was not seriously involved with a woman.[14] His letters throughout his life speak of "home"; but although he did finally marry Ingeborg Weeke in 1898, he never established a family life in any traditional sense. It was an irony to him. In a letter to Ellen Key from 1897 he wrote:

It's a strange arrangement that precisely *I,* in whom the strongest need is a need for *home*, the need to live hidden, distant like all the others who disappear in the crowd, love and be with the same people through the years, eat the same dishes, sit in the same chairs,—that *I* have become this pilgrim, and have become a known person.[15]

In a lighthearted poem written in Paris in 1892, "Når jeg engang gifter mig"[When I Do Get Married, I:87–89], Obstfelder's poet indulges in his most middle class fantasy: a church wedding, not a civil ceremony "like other radicals," a "patented wife," i.e., one who will be only his and who will give him not only herself but children, too, and courage when he needs it. Most importantly they will give each other a home—"our own home,/our own home"—toward which they set off to the sound of church bells.

A much more significant poem inspired by the bourgeois dream is "Genre" (I:31–32), also from the fall of 1892. It is one of the poems from Gent where Obstfelder first felt his poetic gift coming alive again. The poet, who is both husband and father, stands back in awe, watching his sleeping wife and child, "the big beauty" and "the little beauty." The scene is simple in the extreme. It is night. A parafin lamp full of yellow oil burns inside the room, the curtain is open, and a gas lamp burns outside. The poet notices how "mournfully it flickers." Imagining that it is trying to peer at his wife's naked shoulder, he pulls down the curtain so the street lamp's profane view is cut off. No one and nothing must be allowed to see "my white possession," his sleeping wife, a pure and sacred being to him. Yet he ends the poem wondering why they are not always as they should be toward each other, the fantasy ever so gently disturbed by thoughts of reality.

But a closer reading of "Genre" shows that this poem, too, is marked by the melancholy of the 1890s. The eerie simplicity of the scene—the black of the night, the white of the woman, the yellow lamps inside and out like huge eyes glowing in the dark—evokes that sense of mystery in which death waits. Time seems frozen in this room. The wife and the child sleep, the wife like a marble statue; the only movement is of the wick floating "innocently" in the oil of the lamp and the mournful flicker of the gas light. In spite of his treasure, the "whiteness" that is his, the poet is alone in the night, projecting his feelings of loneliness and of being "outside" on the one object that actually is outside, the street lamp. It seems to be his own flickering, melancholy eye.

Obstfelder put on and took off the bourgeois mask, but there was always something not quite right about it, as if it were an impossible fantasy. Significantly in "Genre" the poet does not act as husband and father but more as a timid lover who wants to "sneak quietly up" to his wife and warm himself there. In the earlier erotic poetry, such as "Drinking Song," the woman or the poet slept, allowing him to avoid any confrontation with her and himself remain a child. In "Genre," even when protected by the middle-class ideal of marriage and family, the poet prefers to watch the woman in sleep.

The aspect of the bourgeois ideal that is, in fact, most real to Obstfelder's poet vis-à-vis the woman is the role of the child who finds comfort in the arms of its mother. The "other" child in "Genre" is mentioned only once, then quickly forgotten as if inconsequential to the scene. Children do appear, particularly in the prose, but as George Schoolfield wrote in his article on Obstfelder's works which appeared in *Edda* in 1957:

The child often appears, but a ghostly one, sneaking in and out of the pages as if it had no right to existence. . . . Obstfelder does not allow the child to appear as a developed and influential figure in his works . . . it is present only as a facet of womanhood . . . he fears its coming may destroy his place in his beloved's, its mother's, arms.[16]

In the prose poem "The Belly," the poet even fears and identifies with the fetus growing inside his wife's womb, as if that new life will be the destruction of his own.

The Motherless Child

In "Julaften" [Christmas Eve, I:14–15] Obstfelder portrayed the poet as the motherless child, a metaphor for the outsider who will forever be excluded from the common community. Probably written in December 1892 in Stavanger,[17] it is one of Obstfelder's classic poems both in content and form and, as such, deserves a longer analysis. Typically naive in tone and simple in structure, it is nevertheless a poem of multiple meanings. As much as any of Obstfelder's poems, it presents his interpretation of the individual in the modern world. The myth of the man/child terrified by life— associated both with Obstfelder's private and poetic personae—grew out of the poems like "Christmas Eve."

Like "Agony," "Alone," and "All Creation Sighs," "Christmas Eve" is divided into scenes expressive of variations in the poet's moods. Here, however, there are no dramatic reversals but rather a movement toward alleviation of his despair as he attempts to exert some control over his world. The poem begins with his exclamation that it is Christmas Eve, but only in the second verse do we realize that he is excluded from the warmth and abundance of the festival.

> Christmas Eve!
> Windows bright with Christmas candles,
> trees overflowing living rooms,
> carols through cracks in doors.
>
> I wander streets alone
> listening to children's songs.
> I rest on steps, I think
> of my dead mother.

The contrast is absolute between the children singing carols in the brightness and warmth of the indoors and the poet, wandering alone in the darkness, who identifies with them. They have the things that are the rights of children, i.e., protection, warmth, a home. He is utterly homeless in both a physical and metaphysical sense. He walks the empty streets and sits outside others' homes. Though a grown man, he is the motherless child.

The thoughts of mother and child coupled with the image of Christmas vaguely allude to the Christian virgin and child, making an implicit contrast to the secular Christmas imagery of the first stanza. Religious imagery, it becomes clear, underlies the poem, giving the illusion of a spiritual world behind the real world of loneliness and dark. But the imagery proves to be merely suggestive. It is in the end fragmentary and of no comfort.

In part two the poet leaves the city to seek out a landscape more befitting his mood, one very much like the snow-covered landscape of death in "Agony."

> I walk to the fields—
> out—among the stars.

My shadow glides over shadows
of dead-limbed trees.

I find in the snow,
glittering like Christmas candles,
a body still trembling,
a sparrow, dead of frost.

The stark imagery of the snow-covered fields is even more of a contrast to the warm living rooms than were the empty streets still echoing with the voices of children. The bright candles of the first stanza are carried over into this land of death, but these candles are of snow and give no warmth; and the poet/child, like the sparrow, is dying, but of a spiritual chill.

Religious imagery seems once again implicit in the symbols. The dead-limbed trees may suggest the cross of the martyred Christ, already linked to the poet as the child of Christmas. The dead bird may call to mind the words of Christ that not a single sparrow shall fall to earth without the knowledge of God. The allusions invite questions. Is there salvation from this darkness? Is the poet seen by God? Or is his isolation total?

In part three the scene changes once again to the poet's attic room, sparsely furnished and far above the full living rooms of the community. The structure of the verse changes as well, the poet using a stricter, two line metrical pattern—reminiscent of a children's jingle—in contrast to the more proselike verse of the earlier sections. Two translations of the last section are given, the first a literal translation upon which the interpretation is based, the second a "good" translation which better conveys the tone of the original.[18]

And I went home to my attic room
and put a candle in my bottle.

I put the candle in my bottle
and lay the Bible on my trunk.

I knelt down at my trunk
and blew the dust from my Bible.

I folded my hands over my Bible
and cried.

And I come home
and light the candle.

I place the Bible
on my bed.

I kneel down,
I dust off my Bible.

I fold my hands
and cry.

The poet retreats from the city streets and snow-covered death fields
into his own room, completely isolated and self-contained, and
symbolic of his retreat into himself. As if in a final attempt to stave off
despair, he tries to create some order and to assert some control over
this small world. Ironically, the ways he chooses are the ways of a
child, stereotypically the least in control. He carefully arranges his few
possessions—the candle, the bottle, the trunk, and the Bible—into a
makeshift altar at which he kneels, folds his hands, and cries. He
repeatedly marks the objects around him with the possessive pronoun.
Significantly, in the first sections of the poem only his shadow belonged
to him. Just as he resorts to the more rigid meter of the jingle, he
names and arranges the few things which serve to define him and thus
to protect him from ultimate loneliness, i.e., the loss of self or death.

He also kneels down to pray like a child begging God "his soul to
keep" from the powers of darkness. But although he finds some
emotional release and is able to cry, he is denied metaphysical comfort.
He kneels at an altar of death, the word for "trunk" (*kiste*) meaning
both chest and coffin. The ritual itself is incomplete: the Bible remains
unopened, he cries but he does not pray. (The truncated last line
stylistically reflects this same incompleteness.)

The religious allusions in the earlier sections of the poem implied
the possibility of a spiritual world beyond this one; but such a
possibility seems denied by the emptiness of the ritual. If there is
another world, the poet is unable to reach it. Communication outward
is impossible. There is no one in the streets, his mother is dead, and he
is unable to pray.

The precariousness of the poet's existence is captured in his candle which draws meaning from the candles of part one—life—and the snow candles of part two—death. His own encompasses both, burning as a sign of life, but burning ominously. It is only one, in contrast to the many Christmas candles and sparkles in the snow. Of light it can give only little and of warmth none.

The image of the man as child is one that Obstfelder used often to portray the individual in an alienating world in which the despair is profound and the control minimal. The longing for the mother is itself often an expression for the longing for a spiritual home, for peace, and the reconciliation of the self to the world. In "Christmas Eve" no such reconciliation takes place, although the poet's tears may momentarily ease his fear. In the poems that follow the poet participates in various tableaux of mother and child, longing to be protected from his growing sense of alienation.

The Feminine Cosmos

The woman assumes a powerful cosmic role in relation to the poet's child persona. She appears as a mother goddess in the earlier works as well as the later. In poems from 1890 like "Tempest" and "All Creation Sighs" the universe itself is such a goddess. In the poem "Nocturne" (I:38–39), from 1893, she seems to be the Catholic Virgin Mary, who is rocking all her children to sleep.[19] "A woman hovers out in the blue,/ the Lord's mother, Maria, Maria,/ lovingly shutting the eyes of the soul,/ carefully rocking the cradle of earth." In the Whitmanesque "Pampassange" [Songs of Pampas, I:55–58], also written in 1893,[20] she is the Indian goddess of the earth, "the earth's breast from which sighs rise to the stars," protectress of the night, the day, and of earth's children. In *A Cleric's Journal* she appears in a vision of sun and roses, bringing peace to the tortured priest.[21]

The woman, however, is a goddess of both good and evil, life and death. As in the poems from 1890, she becomes the poet's universe; but in the best of the poems from this time she symbolizes a universe which is both life-giving and life-destroying.

The following poems are all closely linked to the Symbolist concept of the "blue abyss," which Balakian has defined as the frontier between the visible and the invisible, the conscious and the unconscious, non-life and the living. . . . how far one can push beyond the accepted frontier and still come back to write about it became the foremost poetic question after Baudelaire.[22]

Through landscapes shaped and colored by his moods, the poet conveys his feelings of loneliness, alienation, and despair. The poem entitled "Without Name" takes place in a pitch black park in which black leaves fall silently to the ground and gas lamps stare like dilating yellow pupils into the night. In "Eve" the entire landscape—as far as the poet's eye can see—is the same undifferentiated leaden gray, and in "Barcarole" sea and sky flow together in a silent, liquid universe.

At the same time, in each of these poems the mood of the landscape is made inseparable from the central symbol, the mothering woman to whom the poet goes for comfort, giving rise to the paradox that the woman is both goddess and devil. For although she embraces the poet, providing him with a place of refuge from his despair, she is also the very symbol of that despair and envelops him in it.

These are poems that Hannevik would include under the mystical experiences of a meditative character, ". . . filled with chilling, cosmic visions and [occurring] in connection with the white stars, 'the blue,' night, and a dreamy, lyrical and passive eroticism."[23]

"Navnløs" [Without Name, I:9–10][24] opens onto a park bathed in fog and darkness.

> Fogs of darkness fall over trees, on the ground,
> the leaves have no colors, the grass has no green.
> Lanterns flicker, yellow pupils of the dark—
> yellow pupils, widening so mysteriously.
> There is no one, laughing or sighing in the corridors of the park.
> I cough, like a ghost clearing its throat.
> I walk, like a ghost walking.

There is no movement in the park but for the falling leaves, no color save for the eerie yellow lantern eyes, no sound but the cough of the sick poet coming from deep within the dark, undefined space of the park.

In the next stanza the poet seeks out the very heart of this darkness,

In the next stanza the poet seeks out the very heart of this darkness, finding in the innermost corridor a "whore" veiled in black, her mysterious eyes penetrating the darkness like the yellow pupils of the lanterns. Gripped by "a mournful, nocturnal joy,/ to meet in the darkness, in the dead night, a human being," he sits quietly down beside the woman, draws her veil aside and brings his "eyes close to hers," his "soul close to hers."

This meeting between whore and poet, sickly of soul, is undoubtedly meant to be a meeting between two of society's outcasts, she by virtue of the weakness of her flesh, he by virtue of the weakness of his spirit. Hannevik wrote, "She is an anonymous practitioner of the most despised female profession; he is plagued by an 'angst-ridden depression' which borders on insanity. Both are outside the human community. . . ."[25] He calls her first whore, then a human being, but treats her in fact as the former. She sits silently and passively as he draws his body close to hers, seemingly in a lovers' embrace. But instead he lays his head on her breast and begins to cry as if she were his mother and he the saddest of all her small children. "Crying, crying, not knowing why I'm crying." Almost surprised, he says: "She does not push me away./ She gently dries my eyes./ And I grip her hands in somber agony/ and beg her to hide me, hide me, hide me."

When, in the final verse of the poem, the poet repeats his original description of the park, the darkness, once undefined, now seems to be a feminine form "protectively" enveloping the park. Indeed, the woman *is* a protectress in this poem. She not only hides the poet in her arms and soothes his pain but enables him to step outside himself and the tableau he has created. In a very real sense she saves him from being overwhelmed by the darkness of his own mood, allowing him to distance himself from it. Yet at the same time, as the very embodiment of the darkness, she traps him in her arms.

In "Without Name" as well as "Eve" and "Barcarole" which follow, the poet, envisioning himself in an amorphous universe of fog or darkness or endless gray, projects onto this universe a feminine form which can most easily be understood in terms of Jung's formulation of anima. "Every man carries within himself an eternal image of woman, not the image of this or that definite woman, but rather a definite feminine image."[26] Although a further speculation by Jung may be somewhat subjective, it seems particularly appropriate as a description of the relationship Obstfelder's poet feels between the emptiness outside him and the feminine within and vice-versa. "Emptiness is a great feminine mystery. It represents to man the absolutely 'strange,' the yawning hollow, the unfathomable 'other,' the Yin."[27]

This feminine cosmos is an eerie place, cold, passive, and deathlike. In the next poem "Eva" [Eve, I:5–6], the poet finds no relief or warmth. The only comfort Eve is able to provide is the constancy of her ambivalent presence. The poem opens with the poet drawing a simple parallel between the lead gray color of the sea, the sky, and the eyes of the silent woman who sits gripping his hands. It is her eyes, surrounded by silence in the poem, that truly fascinate him. "—Your eyes—/ blue, when the sun laughed and the sea sang!/ You are like nature itself, Eve." He seems to search in her eyes for something other than the emptiness within and without him, but Eve is a terrifying surprise.

> Your lips, resting on my forehead,
> are so cold.
> Your hands, resting in mine,
> are so cold.
> Your breast breathes so heavily,
> —earth's breath against my soul!
>
> You are like earth.
> When sun-mist swims on sun-mist
> sun-mist veils your eye,—
> when fog embraces fog,
> your eye is dark and wet.

Eve is no more and no less than what the poet literally sees before him. She holds no meanings, no secrets, no promises of another world. She is merely a secondary reflection of this one, empty and inconstant.

More so than the woman in "Without Name" Eve is dangerous to this man. The tableau of the corpselike lovers is striking, she sitting somewhat above him, kissing his forehead, breathing coldly and heavily against him. Although she is his only companion in all the emptiness, she is simultaneously the essence of it. She is of life and of the earth, and she is chilling the poet to death. He resigns himself to sitting silently with her, staring into the "fog's anxious night," listening to the "aching sigh of the sea." The poem ends as he cries out her name, "Eve. . . ." Is it a protest against all that she is not? A pathetic cry for help? Recognition that there is nothing more? It is, at any rate, not an ending of any sort, but rather a scream into nothing.

This leaden world of Eve's in which the poet is trapped is one of the most ominous pictures of the "abyss" in Obstfelder's poetry. The poet's cry of Eve's name is the only sign of life. But the poet goes even one step farther in the next poem, "Barcarole," where we seem to have passed beyond the "frontier" into the land of the nonliving. It is a supremely peaceful poem from which *all* deadly emotions are banished, but its benign universe is far more threatening than it might at first seem.

"Barcarole" (I:39–40) is another of the poems from Gent, Belgium. It is as sheer, soft, and gentle as the silent sea it describes, and its language is as musical as any Obstfelder ever wrote. It is a love poem to the woman Elvi, who lies with the poet in a boat gliding silently in the sea. "Watch!" he says to her, "that my soul is not/ hurt."

But the poem is, in fact, a beautiful death wish. The poet deliberately calls for the shadows to fall so that he may hide and sleep in this boat gliding in the night sea. "Concealing shadows,/ sink down!/ as the boat silently/ glides." He commands all the world to be still so that he and Elvi can be alone in their blue universe. He longs to sleep in Elvi's hair. "Here, in your deep/ hair-river./ And your cheek to mine./ Hide me!/ Here I'll sleep—/ long./ As the moon silently/ glides."

Of the three poems the interplay in "Barcarole" between the mood-landscape and the woman is the most diffuse and shifting; yet of all the women Elvi becomes the most all-encompassing, by the end of the poem taking up into her name the boat, the river, the sea, and the sky. *Elv* in Norwegian means "river"; *elvi* in Obstfelder's native dialect means "the river." Thus the water in which the boat glides is not only associated with Elvi but deliberately made inseparable from her again and again. By means of this ambiguity the symbol of Elvi continually changes meaning, all the liquid substances surrounding the poet—the sea, the waves, the river, and the ocean—finally flowing together in her name, through her the entire universe taking on a feminine form that gently rocks, cradles, and protects the child/poet who lies within it. His infantile wish to hide and sleep in this womblike liquid world strongly pulls him away from life into the land of the nonliving. Of all the poems "Barcarole" is the most ill-omened because the poet no longer recognizes any danger. He simply seems to long to be carried passively into death.

These poems are the reverse side of earlier poems like "Tempest" and "All Creation Sighs" in which the poet actively tries to lose himself in a primitive celebration of life. In these poems, too, the poet wishes to lose himself, but he expresses it as a strong wish to be totally passive, metaphorically to cry or to fall asleep in his mother's imprisoning arms.

The Wrong Planet

The pervasive anxiety of so much of Obstfelder's poetry was undeniably a reaction to the growing sense of alienation felt in many quarters of late nineteenth-century society. Speaking both specifically of Obstfelder and more generally of his time, Rolf Nyboe Nettum wrote:

Without the poets interpreting it such themselves—they understand angst as something inexplicable, metaphysically determined, or psychically conditioned—the general reaction must have something to do with the development of society. It is the distancing, the almost unnoticeable stress, the feeling of rootlessness that breaks out.[28]

"Jeg ser"[I See, I:8], written sometime in 1892,[29] is the best-known and, according to many, the finest of Obstfelder's poems. In the context of the expressionistic mood poems discussed in the previous section, "I See" is somewhat unusual in that its landscape is the city and further there is no dominant feminine presence. The poet stands alone and unprotected in the city street, his vision—his only real connection with the outside world—threatened by an impending storm. "I See" shares a significant relationship with the poems that stand before and after it in *Poems*. "Tempest," in which the poet desperately tries to participate in life through reconstruction of a natural orgy, precedes the poem. In "I See" the poet feels himself a foreigner, unable to make contact with anything. He looks and stares but sees nothing. "Without Name" follows, as if the darkness of the storm has descended, and the poet rushes into it to hide his eyes and cry in the arms of his goddess. The tentative reconciliation of the self to the world achieved in "Tempest" he seeks once again in the death park of "Without Name." No such reconciliation seems possible in "I See." The entire poem follows in two translations, the first again a literal translation upon which the interpretation is based, the second a suggestion for a "good" translation.[30]

I see the white sky,
I see the gray-blue clouds,
I see the bloody sun.

So this is the world
So this is the home of the planets.

A rain drop!

I see the tall buildings.
I see the thousands of windows,
I see the distant church tower.

So this is the earth.
So this is the home of mankind.

The gray-blue clouds gather.
The sun is gone.

I see the well-dressed gentlemen,
I see the smiling ladies,
I see the bowed horses.

The lead blue clouds grow heavy.

I see, I see. . .
I must have come to the wrong planet!
It's so strange here. . .

I see white sky,
I see gray blue clouds,
I see blood red sun.

So this is the world,
so this is home for the planets.

A drop of rain!

I see tall buildings,
thousands of windows,
a distant church tower.

So this is earth,
this is the home of man.

Lead blue clouds gather.
The sun is gone.

I see well-dressed gentlemen,
I see smiling ladies,
stooped horses.

The leaden clouds grow heavy.

I look, I look. . .
This must be the wrong planet!
I'm a stranger here. . .

In this early piece of poetic science fiction the poet, with a mixture of detachment and disbelief, stands in the middle of the city, looking upward toward an eerie sky, white with lead-blue clouds and a bloodied sun. As the storm gathers his vision is weighted continually downward, past the tall buildings, to the men and women in the streets, to the stooped horses, until he too is bowed, staring at the ground of this strange alien place. He is imprisoned in a world of fragmented, impenetrable surfaces—the buildings are seen as facades, the windows do not look into anything, the men and women are defined by their city costumes and smiling masks—and the only thing holding these surfaces together is the descending vertical line of his own sight, imperiled by the storm. At the end of the poem he repeats, as if he were paralyzed, "I see, I see" or "I look, I look"—both meanings are contained in the Norwegian *ser*—but he perceives nothing, apparently losing even his visual grasp on the objects and colors in the world around him. The gray storm seriously threatens his vision, i.e., his sight, his understanding, and his perspective. He is even unable to complete the last line of the poem.

The poem is masterfully composed, its structural disintegration paralleling the poet's loss of vision. It is divided into three sections of three stanzas each: the first two are mirror images of each other—three lines, two lines, one line—but the pattern is broken in the last section into three lines, one line, three lines. Just as there are three sections, there are also three distinctly different themes or, more precisely, mental activities performed by the poet: he groups the objects in the world around him into visual images of the sky, the city, and the city's inhabitants; he interprets *what* he sees on the basis of what he *expects* to see, i.e., the "home of the planets" and "the home of mankind"; and he registers the progress of the storm. But toward the end of the poem, instead of following his pattern of composing a visual image and then interpreting it immediately, he notices how heavy the clouds are growing, as if he were growing more disoriented and losing his train of thought. Further, the last stanza, which should—following the pattern—contain the poet's interpretation of what he sees, is actually an ironic combination of themes one and two, i.e., he looks but sees nothing and knows that this world, rather than any kind of home for him, is the wrong planet.

Overemphasis of the movement in the poem toward alienation and loss of control would be misleading, as it would suggest that the poet initially exercised more control and felt more "at home" than he actually does. As Asbjørn Bergaas has pointed out, there is only the very weakest relationship between the poet and the images he perceives.

Every single image is presented as an independent entity and as mutually isolated phenomena—no relationship is established from image to image, only from the "I" as the center to isolated points outside it. . . . We would have had a surer grasp of the poet's emotional reaction to the visual sensations if instead of "the *white* sky" it had said "the *pure* sky," if "the *gray blue* clouds" were "the *threatening* clouds". . . the I finds himself in such an impersonal relationship to his surroundings that they are registered as purely visual sensations.[31]

The degree of alienation the poet feels in "I See" can be gauged by looking back to two of the more joyful poems of 1890, "Rain" and "Spring." The poet was so in touch with his world then that he could physically feel it. In "Rain" he was content merely to convey the properties of the marvelous natural phenomenon, but in "I See" he is so distanced from the storm that he can barely comprehend it. The single drop of rain seems to startle him, as if momentarily jolting him out of his trance. In "Spring" everything from wine to women to words and sounds delighted the poet. He invented them, controlled them, played with them, shaping his world to fit his idea of what he would like it to be. The joy of life he felt in "Spring" is replaced in "I See" by a paralyzing detachment, the things he sees about him no longer toys for his pleasure but surfaces that have little to do with him. His words, earlier a real source of inspiration, are now a monotonous litany of disinterested observations. "I see, I see," he repeats over and over again.

It would be misleading to imply through a comparison of "Spring" and "I See" a development in Obstfelder's poetry from joy in life to alienation. His moods, the prime determinants in his work, were cyclical, and therefore a comparison of the two poems most correctly conveys the emotional extremes found in his poetry.

The same is true of his work in general. Some things were written more under the influence of a certain mood than others, of course, but it is the fluctuation in mood that is constant.

Neither is there any major philosophical development. It is generally accepted that Obstfelder emerged from his breakdown with a belief in a personal God.[32] This may indeed be true, but it did not generate any *fundamental* change. The concept of a superior being is to be found in his writing both before and after 1891. Obstfelder always had a mystic's yearning to "see God," whether he defined it as a raging storm, or a spiral of light and fire, or the Christian God. Nor does his writing indicate that he ever had an unshaken belief in such a God. Often, as in "Christmas Eve," there is no divine presence, only a desperate longing for one; and in poems like "Eve" the longing itself is rendered meaningless. Again, doubt and longing are the constants in Obstfelder's works, not belief. The mood, of course, is often religious, but dogma is hard to detect.

Development in his authorship must be viewed in terms of experimentation with various forms. Already in 1892 he had written to his brother regarding some of his poems: "They don't satisfy me. . . . when one has something original to say it takes a long time to find the form."[33] In retrospect we know he found it in the prose poem.

Chapter Four

The Prose Poems

The Form

Obstfelder's prose poems, only twenty-five in number in the collected works, comprise a small but superior part of his writing.[1] The darling genre of many of the poets of the 1890s, the prose poem was also a favorite of Obstfelder's. His earliest prose pieces were written in the late 1880s, but he probably did not seriously experiment with the form until the fall of 1892, when he met Thiis in Paris, the home of the masters of the prose poem, Baudelaire, Mallarmé, and Rimbaud. He wrote the majority of these poems between 1892 and 1894.[2]

The free, short form was well suited to Obstfelder's talent and artistic aims. He seems to have recognized in it the same possibilities as Baudelaire. Linking the two poets, Hannevik has written:

Baudelaire's program for this new and difficultly defined genre had to appeal to a writer like Obstfelder. About the prose poem the French poet wrote: "Who of us is there who has not, in ambitious moments, dreamt about the revelation of a poetic prose, musical without rhythm and rhyme, sufficiently supple and sufficiently flexible to subordinate itself to the lyrical rapids of the soul, the fluctuations of the dream, the spasmodic springs in consciousness."[3]

At his best, Obstfelder achieved Baudelaire's "ambitious" dream of a language both musical and sufficiently supple. Reidar Ekner used the Swedish term *mjuk*—meaning both soft and supple—to describe his language, the "softness" deriving most importantly, in Ekner's estimation, from the infrequent number of accented syllables.[4] The prose poem allowed Obstfelder to use more freely the deceptively simple poetic language he had striven for in his poetry in verse, a necessarily more restrictive medium.

The prose poem's undefined form also easily lent itself to the conveyance of his intense moods. He could, first of all, make the poem as short as he wished; and, indeed, in many of them he proved Poe right in his assertion that "all intense excitements are, through a psychal necessity, brief."[5] Also the poem did not have to function according to any fixed structure: there need be no beginning, middle, and end; other than logical or sequential relationships could bind one thought to the next; and the open or questioning ending which Obstfelder so often used provided a fitting "closure." Such freedom was an obvious advantage to a poet like Obstfelder who was trying to express new and still unanalyzed structures of mood, dreams, and the unconscious.

If he worked with any one structural pattern, it was a fugue-like structure—common already to the poetry in verse—based on the statement, repetition, and variation of themes. One of the most obvious applications of the structure in the prose poems can be seen in "Roser" [Roses, II:238–41], originally composed in 1886 and rewritten in 1892. This rather long poem is like a dream in which the dreamer feels himself being buried in "roses and red and rose petals covered with snow." Three major themes repeat themselves, sometimes separately, sometimes in combination with each other. The first is the poet's physical sensation of being covered in roses.

> *Massing* over him, falling, trickling, trickling,
> hurling, piling up, massing over him into a soft—
> white petals, red petals—soft rosekiss, rosepetalkiss.
> On his forehead, on his mouth, on his throat.

The second theme is the poet's wish to die in the arms of a mother figure whom he connects with the roses, and the third is his erotic fantasy of the woman and himself, their hearts beating together as they seem to merge into one.

> There are *two*. There are *two*.
> It's dying.
> There are *two*. There are *two*.
> Dying.
> *
> One.

These three major themes state themselves, disappear, and are variously transformed as in a dream. At the end of the poem Obstfelder attempts to bring them together in harmony and then allows them to separate and fade as the dreamer loses his sense of oneness with the woman and the roses. He even employs musical terminology to orchestrate the poem.

> No sky, no stars, but a high sea—of roses—and
> beyond the edge of roses, more—roses.
> The heart slows, becomes a—rose—withering.
> Sap dries up. Petals shrink.
> Wildly out toward the horizon, roses, he stares
> wildly, wildly, roses, roses, rosepetals (furioso),
> rosebuds :/: roseleaves :/: roseperfume, rosetears, rose—
> rosecolors,—(mor.) roses.
>
> *
>
> I?
>
> *
>
> He stares wildly out toward the horizon, out toward—
> roses.
>
> Dying
> *   *
> *
> You?

The "musical structure" is seldom as transparent as in "Roses"; nevertheless, most of the poems function according to this principle of recurring themes, which, for Obstfelder, was a fundamental principle of life. In the "America Journal" he wrote:

This, that changes tempo, this, that grows in strength, this, that suddenly stops, and thinks, this that returns, continually returns as something else, in another form perhaps, weaker, stronger, becomes the principal voice,—all this is found in life. Fugued music is found in nature. (III:154)

In particular, the loose structure lent itself to the kind of indirect communication Obstfelder hoped might reveal "the inexpressible." Repeated words could gradually take on new meanings, repeated themes could be treated several times to bring out as many nuances as possible, various themes could be dialectically structured to bring out their meanings both in opposition and in contrast to each other.

The single most important technique used by Obstfelder in the prose poems was made possible by this structure based on repetition. The technique can best be described as the conscious withholding of information from the reader in order to create a strange or mysterious mood. More information is gradually supplied as certain themes are returned to, but only partially and usually after the fact, again heightening the mood.

In his book *The Techniques of Strangeness in Symbolist Poetry,* James Kugel showed that the quality of strangeness (or mystery) that has become the hallmark of a Symbolist poem is achieved primarily through this device of withholding information. Kugel wrote:

> . . . the poem . . . has a certain aura of mystery about it, due to the "missing information" which, it is implied, is necessary for full comprehension. In other words, the poet creates the strangeness by *not telling everything,* or more precisely, by implying that not everything has been told.[6]

Kugel included an anthology of Symbolist devices for withholding information: allusion to proper names without gloss or elucidating context, implying the person referred to is known to the reader; apparent reference to an unknown story or symbolic value; lack of comprehensible motive; and any number of others.[7] Obstfelder used these and similar devices, in his own way, in everything he wrote; but there is no doubt that he was most successful in the prose poems.

In one sense, he was never more in the mainstream of the European Symbolist movement, but in another, he desired different ends. Kugel maintained that with mysteriousness the poets created a barrier between themselves and the world.

> For, in the poetry of strangeness the relationship between poet and reader also contains a barrier: a Symbolist poem cannot be "what oft was thought but ne'er so well expressed," but is, rather, something foreign, something which never wholly becomes the reader's own. To be mysterious is to express separation and disjunction. . . .[8]

Although a sense of isolation and alienation is often the effect of much of Obstfelder's poetry, he nevertheless saw in the quality of mysteriousness the *possibility* of the opposite, i.e., the possibility to communicate precisely because not all is defined. Obstfelder believed in what T. S. Eliot would call the "objective correlative." The poet writes subjectively and the reader receives and interprets subjectively; but on a deeper level they communicate the psychological or emotional truth that has inspired their subjective interpretations. As personal or as strange as many of the prose poems are, they communicate with a psychological universality both remarkable and often disturbing.

The Wine of Depression

Like the poems in verse, many of the prose poems deal with the fears and anxieties of depression. Obstfelder had a surprisingly sophisticated understanding of its poisonous effects. In a poem first published by Reidar Ekner in *A Strange Fellowship*, he wrote:

> The wine of depression is strange, its alcohol bubbles in the blood and poisons vitality. Laughter turns into the scornful howl of little demons. Sorrow flutters in the warm, pure winter air that burns so loyally with its few rays of sun that the snow melts.
>
> ....
>
> He who drinks the wine of bitterness hurries away; everything about him is strange, his name, his clothes, his ideas. I wonder if you too think I am strange, I don't understand it, you avoid me. I'm so tired.[9]

Obstfelder wrote the majority of these angst-ridden poems during the winter of 1893–1894, which he spent in Copenhagen. Even though *Poems* was published in December and his reputation as an author was established, his spirit was more troubled than at any time since his release from Frogner Colony. In letters to his brother and friends he wrote of recurring anxiety and of the fear that he would never be able to enjoy life. He complained to one friend of periods of unconquerable depression which left him indifferent to everything.[10] And he repeatedly wrote of feelings of self-loathing: ". . . my organism is ugly and sick. . . I think I'm disgusting."[11] "There are times when I feel I am lower than the crawling worm. . . ."[12]

The extreme depression of this period must have been partially self-induced. Obstfelder was deliberately trying to recall the illusions and hallucinations that tortured him during his mental breakdown in order to write a book about them. Even *during* the breakdown he had been conscious of the psychic and symbolic value of his hallucinations. He wrote in the Frogner letter to his brother that his sickness had taken the form of

an unending, terribly strenuous battle against illusions, with at the same time, painful attempts to hold on to the illusions in the course of the illness and extract from them the psychic (spiritual) truth they must at least periodically contain.[13]

Time allowed him to forget and/or repress much in the months that followed, including the Frogner letter; but already in the summer of 1893 he wrote to his brother about the book he intended to write and in September he asked him to send the letter to him. "You understand that I need those things I can get from the time of the fresh wounds."[14] The book he spoke of in fact became *A Cleric's Journal*. But as Brodwall was the first to point out, he also made use of his recorded hallucinations and symbol images in a number of poems in verse and prose. For example, the Indian imagery in "The Songs of Pampas" and the yellow butterfly in the prose poem "Husfru" [Housewife], which will be discussed later, originally occur in writings from that time. In consciously calling up his deeply troubled memories, Obstfelder inevitably called up the accompanying depression.

But not all the dark poems to be discussed here were written during the winter months of 1893–1894. "Genre" was one of the first poems Obstfelder wrote in the fall of 1892 while traveling with Thiis, and "The Dog" from 1900 was one of his last poems. Neither do all these poems contain images directly traceable to his illness. But there is an amazing similarity—in form and emotional intensity—between these poems and hallucinations and nightmares in general. Brodwall, in fact, was so impressed with the similarity that he was skeptical that Obstfelder could have written much of what he did without having actually experienced it.

Hallucinations occur several places in Obstfelder's work. He uses them well and seems to have a remarkable understanding of their nature. If he as an author wanted to make use of such means without having first hand knowledge of them, he would most likely have revealed his more superficial knowledge in one way or another.[15]

The precise relationship between these poems of angst and depression and Obstfelder's personal history remains an unknown. Artistically they are some of his best poems, leading to the conclusion that he did indeed learn a great deal from studying the nature of the dreams and hallucinations of madness. The intensity of emotion, the tendency to give such feeling a physical form, the confusion of thought, fantasy, and reality all contribute to the hypnotic brilliance of this group of poems.

Obstfelder's technique in the prose poems in general can best be demonstrated through one of the poems in particular. "Bugen" [The Belly, II:264–65], written during the Copenhagen winter, is an excellent example. Its theme of entrapment is central to these dark poems, and it shares various formal elements with the others as well: the repetition of phrases and themes, the combination of realistic and abstract elements, and the conscious ambiguity—or, in Baudelaire's words, the "delicious obscurity"[16]—achieved by the withholding of information from the reader. The entire text of "The Belly" follows.

> A whisper, "Smother me."
> Like the hot scirocco from the black abyss.
> Then a pause, long fatigue and soothing darkness
> and two eyes, two eyes with a new sparkle.
> But suddenly she jumps up. She opens the curtain.
> She jumps up in the window. She is naked.
> —"Can you see me?"
> Night in there. Outside day.
> On the woman's swelling belly fall pale morning rays.
> That high, white mass beween night and day, was it
> his wife?
> That hot steaming belly, does it carry his child?
> "Can you see me?"
> And in the cold gray light he sneaks down to the
> docks. Dead fish stink. In the green-gray water he is

met by his own face, idiotic, dead.
Does his child's seed slumber inside in the
swelling, steaming belly?

"The Belly" is a highly emotional poem in which reality merges
into nightmare. Ultimately it must be understood as the poet's external
projection of internal fears. But first of all it is a starkly realistic, visual
tale of a man who awakens in the early hours of the morning, repulsed
and terrified by the presence of his pregnant wife. In disbelief he asks
whether the ominous figure could be his wife and if his child could
really be inside the belly. Apparently to escape the suffocating reality
of the room, he sneaks down to the waterfront, but there he is
confronted once again with the horror of the womb as he stares into
the murky water and sees his own dead face.

Apart from the first two lines of the poem, the tale is told
cinematically—for the most part in black and white—through a series
of sparsely sketched but, at the same time, concrete images that emerge
slowly and fragmented from the darkness, made blacker not by any
descriptive adjectives but through the sense of suffocation called forth
by the words, "smother me." (These are the first words in the original
text.) We "see" first two eyes "with a new sparkle," then a woman's
body, undefined but naked, posing in a window, her large belly
projected against the dim light, then the figure of a man in the streets,
and finally his face mirrored in the green-gray water. Although nearly
colorless, green-gray is, in contrast to the lack of color in the rest of
the poem, strikingly vivid and frightening, by implication describing
not only the water of the harbor but the liquid of the womb. The
imagery is minimal and bold, achieving a visual intensity that both
carries and parallels the emotional complexity of the poem.

Contrary, however, to the concrete, realistic tale—admittedly only
fully apparent after several readings—is the nightmarish obscurity of
"the black abyss" that envelops the poem. Technically the obscurity is
created by telling the tale backwards, or by withholding information,
so that we are never sure what a given piece of information means and
are therefore continually forced to reinterpret what has gone before.
The sense of reality, like the early morning light, is constantly shifting.

The presence of two people, for example, is only gradually apparent, although we suspect that there is *another* who hears the whisper, registers the pause, sees the eyes. But nothing is knowable for certain because the narrative voice itself is ambiguous. The beginning of the poem seems to be told in first person. But when the narrator says "Night in there" rather than "Night in here" confusion arises, for the voice seems to be coming from outside the room, not inside. Perhaps the woman is alone. But then why her apparent question, "Do you see me?"

The next line of the poem—"On the woman's swelling belly fall pale morning rays."—both clarifies and confuses what has gone before. We now understand why the woman has a new sparkle in her eyes, and we can piece together the fragmented images to form a portrait of her, but significantly the most important information—that she is pregnant—has been withheld until last. We must readjust our picture of her in the window as well as reinterpret the meaning of the phrase, "Night in there." The suspicion arises that the narrator, whose identity is still unknown, may be referring to the inside of the womb. "The hot scirocco from the black abyss" takes on a possible new meaning. At the very least we begin to associate the womb with night, suffocation, and despair.

In the next line—"That high, white mass between night and day, was it his wife?"—through the seemingly insignificant possessive pronoun "his," we are given the most important information needed to begin at least partially to understand the confusing first lines of the poem, the relationship between the man and the woman, the man's angst, so present yet so unexplained. Only now is it certain that a man and his pregnant wife are together in the room—although the narrative voice is still ambiguous—and only now can the whisper, the allusion to "the black abyss," the pause and the exhaustion be interpreted with some confidence. Possibly the woman is awaking from sleep troubled by nightmare and physical discomfort; but more likely the man and the woman have made love, or she is, at least, trying to get him to do so. This interpretation best explains the emotional intensity of the beginning of the poem. We also begin to comprehend—but again only partially—the complex psychological sources of the man's disgust and despair: his experience of sexuality as suffocating; his feelings of impotence in his relationship to the woman, full of life, who dominates the room and his vision; and his sense of alienation brought about by the "abnormal" figure of his wife and, most likely, by the disparity he sees between woman as mother and woman as sexual tease, for she seems to taunt him when she seems to say, "Can you see me?"

The next two lines of the poem—"That hot steaming belly, does it carry his child? Can you see me?"—are crucial. For the first time, apart from the very beginning of the poem, adjectives are used that are not emotionally neutral, making us fully aware of the man's real terror of the womb, forcing once again a reinterpretation of what has been seen and how it has been seen. In retrospect the woman's pregnant silhouette grows more ominous, her eyes more taunting, her belly larger, more alive, and more frightening. By the nature of the man's question and the association he makes between the heat of the black abyss and the heat of the womb, it must be understood that he is staring into the womb and that the real reason for his fear is that he sees it as a place of suffocation and death, not life.

Realizing where this man's terrified gaze is directed, we begin to suspect, with some horror, that the question, "Can you see me?" may not be coming from the woman, who seemed the most likely speaker but from the fetus. But now the lines between realistic tale, nightmare, and symbolic poem blur and cannot really be separated, for there is simply not enough information to keep them apart. The narrator has so deliberately confused us, carefully not specifying the speaker of the whisper or the question. The man *may* be listening to the fetus calling out to be seen. The mysterious plea from the beginning of the poem— "smother me"—may be the fetus crying out for its own death before it has known life.

No one final interpretation is possible, meaning turning in upon meaning as the poem comes to a close. The man attempts to escape from the atmosphere of death and suffocation in the room and in the womb—which have become inextricably confused—but as if caught in an ever more encompassing horror, he meets his idiot image in the green-gray water, slumbering there like the fetus in the womb. And now both his and the reader's associations race between life and death, future, past, and present. On a deeply psychological level, by virtue of the identification he makes between the liquids of the womb and the water, he expresses the primitive fear of his own conception and birth, thrown momentarily back upon himself into the far reaches of his unconscious past. But at the same time in the fetus, "his child," he sees the future, hopeless, lifeless before it has even begun. Perhaps it is the man himself, in a desperate appeal to the fragile new life in the belly, who asks, "Can you see me?" His sense of despair and alienation is so intense that such an interpretation cannot be excluded. Perhaps it is the man who cried out, "Smother me," unable to escape the nightmarish vision of the world as "the hot steaming belly." For the belly consumes him, at first blocking his vision to the light outside the window, finally metaphorically enveloping his entire being. Might it not be the man, the poet, who cries out in confusion for both life— "Can you see me?"—and death—"Smother me"?

Like the poet, we are caught within the confusion of the poem: perspectives shift, words and lines take on new meanings in retrospect, questions produce answers which themselves become questions. Obstfelder never rewards us with the clarity or comfort of one final interpretation. The deliberate ambiguity is both technique and metaphor, for in his poetic universe there is little clarity or comfort to be found.

In four out of the five poems from the winter of 1893–1894 the poet's angst expresses itself as horror and disgust of a woman. Unlike the woman who is portrayed as both a redeeming and a threatening presence in the cosmic poems such as "Without Name" and "Barcarole," she is here a terrible and surreal opponent. As in "The Belly"— Obstfelder's ultimate poem about the destructive mother figure—the poet feels trapped by her in both a physical and a metaphysical sense. She has the power to suffocate, to blind, to expose, and to terrorize.

The poem "Den sortklædte" [Dressed in Black, II:265–66], also from the fall of 1893, is as graphic and as nightmarish as "The Belly.' (The same formal elements are present as well—the combination of realism and abstraction, the blurring of the lines between reality and nightmare, withholding information—but they will not be discussed in detail.) The poet is sneaking down a pitch black, empty city street, keeping close to the walls of the buildings. He feels something following him and hears a whisper, "Man." A woman, described only as black "women's clothes," brushes up against him. Suddenly the two are walking up a flight of stairs, then standing under a roof window. She opens her blouse to reveal her breasts, and she says, "Is it beautiful?" impersonally, as if her own body were not a part of her. And the poem ends:

> And she clings to me, and strokes my face, my neck,
> my chest, my whole body. With soft, careful hands.
> And these hands whisper:
> —Blind.

Only through the last word of the poem do we learn that the woman is blind. But immediately the sensuous image of her soft caresses over the man's body changes from a loving to a threatening act. Dressed in black and blind, she seems to smother the poet in darkness with her whispering hands.

The sense of suffocation is very strong in both "The Belly" and "Dressed in Black." Claustrophobic feelings are not uncommon in Obstfelder's writing in general and, although often, they are not always connected with women. The stranger of "I See" feels the storm closing in on him, threatening his vision and possibly his life; and in the "America Journal" a minister is described as afraid to walk, as if "something were resting on him someplace or other" (III:157). In "Genre" (II:251–52), one of the first poems written in the fall of 1892, a woman is the victim of this sense of oppression.

She experiences time and space physically closing in upon her. It is dusk, the hour when one looks into one's own heart, "and that is dangerous, dangerous!" Alone in her house, she decides to play the piano, somehow a symbol of her past. But little things prevent her from playing. First she must light a candle, then raise the piano stool, then she seems to hear something, and locks the door, locking out all the people who talked and laughed so stupidly. It is good one has keys, she says to herself. But having gotten everything ready—as it were, having beautifully prepared her isolation—she still cannot play. She blows out the candle and lies down to think; and a memory as open as her house is closed comes to her.

—the trees and the beach.
Happiness, happiness, warm and wonderful and complete and
I did not take hold of it. The fragrance on the beach and
the seas, the seas,—

But suddenly the flow of the memory is cut off. She is gripped by an anxiety she does not understand. "I have put out the candle, I have closed the door, I lie here so quietly," she says. And the poem ends, "It is just as if someone were standing over me all the time. I feel his warm breath. I dare not open my eyes." This sense of a hovering, threatening presence is common to nightmares that occur in half-sleep; and it is perhaps just such a half-sleep that best describes the mood of this poem. Is it a dream? Is it real? It is impossible to say.

What caused the woman to become so fearful? Perhaps it is the memory of that warm day? Was there a lover who frightened her and now hovers over her in another form? More likely the angst arises from her inability to seize the life she so desires in the past and the present. Her actions—or her inability to act—suggest a paralyzing ennui. Disturbingly, the past is the present, and she locks herself in now as she did then. Her fears oppress her physically, paralyzing her so that she cannot open her eyes.

The sensation of physical oppression accompanied not only moments of angst but also of ecstasy. An image Obstfelder recorded several times in the "America Journal" and one obviously connected with a feeling of being in God's presence is the beating of great wings over his body. "During the nights this year— — I have felt the beating of wings— —rhythms of the beatings of wings, coming nearer, hovering over me,—moving away" (III:164). In the mystical love poem "Roses," the lover feels his head being buried in rose petals, "on his forehead, on his mouth, on his throat" (II:238).

But whether born of ecstasy or angst, such images reveal an extreme passivity. Although he assumes various poetic masks, Obstfelder shows himself over and over again to be overwhelmed by life. The man of "The Belly" is powerless in the presence of his pregnant wife, the man of "Dressed in Black" submits helplessly to the woman's terrifying caresses, the woman of "Genre" simply lies down in fear. The most horrific of these images occurs in *A Cleric's Journal*. The young minister's self-hate assumes a physical form, torturing him in a way disturbingly similar to the falling rose petals.

> Dirty thoughts flutter through the darkness, the thoughts have taken bodies, they have eyes, they have noses, they have claws—they stink, stink.
> There are dirty thoughts, ugly thoughts around me, in all the corners, they fly, they gather closer round me, closer and closer, they lie down on my eyes, they lie down on my tongue, they creep down my throat—oh God,— if you are good,—help, help! (II:125–26)

In another poem from the Copenhagen winter of 1893–1894 the poet is rendered so helpless by his own fears that he goes mad. Hannevik has written of the poem "Natten" [Night, II:266–68)[17]: "It is not so easy to find any clear lines. . . . conflicting impulses simultaneously assert themselves so strongly that the poem's I is completely in their power."[18] The poem at first seems to be the erotic fantasy of a waking man in the night. Like the poet of "Yearning" he dreams of a woman of light and fire. "Why don't you come, life, great, tall woman, and light the thousands of flames in my body, the millions of stars in my blood?"

But when he hears her footsteps he cringes in fear, and his fantasy becomes a nightmare. He is not ready, he cries; his soul does not understand her, does not understand "her eyes in the dark." He seems paralyzed by the sound of her footsteps. Then suddenly the two are walking side by side, apparently in the street. The woman is now a nun dressed in black. She stretches out her hand and looks at him with eyes full of the compassion of the Mother of God and the suffering of the earth. He feels her embrace him and kiss him, "the kiss of the chastized and purified instincts." Only in this "chaste" fantasy can there be any reconciliation between his desire and his fearful disgust. A similar resolution took place in "Agony," the poet finding peace in the metaphor of the virginal morning sun kissing the church tower.

The woman often embodies the greatest danger to the poet's fragile life. But she is, nevertheless, a presence or an *other* through which he can confront himself; and she *can* be transformed into his protectress.

In two of the most haunting prose poems, "The City" from 1893 and "The Dog" from 1900, the woman is absent. The poet's isolation is total and experienced so acutely that he feels under vicious attack.

Isolation, of course, is ironically the state in which Obstfelder's poet feels most secure. His self-image is of a lonely being, set apart and different, and he often seeks isolation as a source of comfort and inspiration.

Such inspirational isolation is nowhere to be found in "Byen" [The City, II:262–64]. The poet, living alone in the mountains, seems nervous and troubled over the absence of people. "Where are they all now? What are they doing? Are they still living? Are my brothers, the people, still living?" He perceives the mountain has no heart and hurries into the valley where "thousands of hearts beat in unison." But once in the city he encounters a nightmare: he hears a scream; the minister is chastizing his people for being rotten and sinful; ridden with angst, the poet runs past a house filled with many people sitting along the walls, not talking or smiling; he runs on past a dance hall where men and women are kicking each other bloody. The communication the poet came to the city to find has turned into its grotesque negative. The church is filled with sadism and self-hate, the houses with surreal silences, and the dance halls have become battle grounds. The poet encounters a deadly breakdown in communication far more harmful to life than the real isolation in the mountains.

"The City" is one of Obstfelder's strongest poetic statements against modern alienation. The alienation of "I See" is threatening though not yet violent, but in "The City" real savagery erupts, a metaphor for the spiritual and emotional violence being done to the self in this world where no one can any longer speak to his neighbor. The minister turns on his congregation, men and women turn on each other, and the individual turns on himself. In the last mad image of the poem the poet hears crying all around him and sees people running past him, whipped by their own shadows. All he is able to say is, "Yes, they're mad, they're mad."

An equally terrifying and perhaps far more personal poem is "Hunden Radering" [The Dog—subtitled "Etching," II:285–89], written in March 1900, five months before Obstfelder's death. The poem—a brutal encounter between a man and a surreal dog—seems clearly to have originated in the hallucinations of his illness. In a letter to Vilhelm Krag, written in the summer of 1892,[19] Obstfelder spoke of the black dog that appears in Krag's prose poem "Night.'

It is just you roaming alone, alone in space, and then the black dog comes——is there any meaning in this black dog that has also been in my soul's, Sigbjørn's soul's history and imprinted itself in words—is there any meaning in it? (III:238)

Brodwall noted that in the Frogner letter Obstfelder wrote of being in death's claws and of having an understanding of evil.[20] In the poem, the dog—a destructive and evil force—leaves a bloody claw mark on the man's hands. There are similarities between this poem and *A Cleric's Journal*, which Obstfelder was working on at the same time, but Hannevik seemed to think that the poem even more so than the "Journal" "revolves around experiences from the time of his insanity."[21]

The narrator tells the tale as if he were reconstructing his own nightmare. At times he speaks in past tense as an observer of the dream. He writes, for example, that it was *as if* he heard strange words coming from the dog's mouth, that he *remembers* seeing the dog's eyes, and that he has since realized—what he did not recognize then—that the dog's astonishment turned to fear. But at other times he speaks in the present tense, as the participant not the observer, and as if all that is happening is real. The deliberate confusion between reality and nightmare seen in other prose poems is masterfully incorporated into both the form and the content of this poem.

The narrator is walking alone, as if in his sleep, over a brown mountain plateau. When he reaches the top he sees a sunset so magnificent that he forgets everything else. But when he comes out of his trance and remembers he must go on, he cannot find his way. He is trapped by an abyss on one side and a steep wall on the other. Dizzy and anxious, he crawls on his knees searching for the path. Just when he thinks he has found it he sees a large dog coming toward him, and he is gripped by angst as he lies clutching the ground. Dog and man lie staring at each other. The man knows the dog will claw his hand

but seems unable to move, and the dog wounds him. Then the man
seems to hear terrible words coming from the dog:

> —Your hour has come, mortal!
> Do you remember what you did? Do you remember you
> whipped me with your twisted whip? Do you remember that?
> Do you remember that you hit my brother the horse
> with pointed scourges, when he sank to the ground in deathly
> fatigue?

The dog blames the man for the killing of life "with his disgusting
white hands" for thousands of years. Though he sees the absurdity of
the accusation, the man at the same time accepts responsibility.

> I knew that I had walked more carefully over the
> earth than most. But the animal did not understand. To
> it I was only a human being, a human being with white,
> murdering hands. And while its eyes stared at me it was
> as if it was me that had whipped and tortured all the
> deathly tired horses of the earth.

The man, so fearful and apparently so full of self-loathing, wishes
the dog would put an end to him. But then inexplicably he feels a
strange power surge through him, and he cries out in wild, nonsense
sounds: "Wéji ohahú! Dilodáma! Wáhi Wóha Wéji ohahú!" He
seems to gain supernatural strength, and the dog, first astonished, then
frightened, disappears. It is as if strength and fear have changed
places, and the man grows stronger and stronger until he is screaming
with the howling wind.

When he comes to his senses the dog is gone, and he is exhausted.
He wonders if he has dreamed it all, but there is a deep, bloody mark
on his hand. When he returns to the hotel people look at him
strangely, which he does not understand until he returns to his room
and looks in the mirror to find that his hair has turned gray.

The meaning of the poem is ambiguous, but it is possible, once
again, to interpret it as an enactment of the poet's exaggerated fears of
entrapment and helplessness growing out of his sense of isolation. It is

from just this situation that his terrible fear, incarnate in the dog, arises. His feelings of helplessness lead to feelings of such unworthiness that he wishes to be destroyed. But something in him inexplicably fights back. The wild sounds he screams save his life. The fear and the dog recede. Paradoxically, out of the primitive fear of the dog the man wins a primitive strength, enabling him to regain himself and be one with the primal life forces as he howls with the storm in an act similar to the raging dance in "Tempest."

Brodwall had a different interpretation. In speaking of Obstfelder's use of neologisms, apparently with "The Dog" in mind, he wrote:

If Obstfelder himself had experienced how neologisms arise, if he had heard them as hallucinations, or used them himself to express something strange he thought or felt, then he knew that it is when one loses control over the psychic functions that such a thing occurs.[22]

Although this may be an accurate explanation of the psychic phenomenon, aesthetically it does not apply equally well to the poem. The man can only regain control by losing it. It seems particularly significant—considering Obstfelder's concern that the poet should express the "inexpressible"—that the man/poet fights back with nonsense words, words that come from the deepest and most *inexpressible* levels of consciousness. Created out of chaos, the words also defend the self against it.

The Sweet Awakening

In contrast to the poems of depression Obstfelder wrote several prose poems about reawakening to life's deep and simple secrets. Although he was not given to moralizing, he allowed himself the luxury of conveying to the reader—quite specifically in the first two poems, more profoundly in the third—that there is sweetness to be found in even the smallest of things if one only knows how to see and dares to enjoy. In each poem a tiny insect aids the human observer in his or her rediscovery of life. "The Worm" and "The Wasp"—dates unknown—are rather precious and of minor importance in themselves, but significant as a contrast to the darker poems. "Housewife," from 1892, is a much more complex and very beautiful poem about the feelings of loss at middle age.[23]

Obstfelder, the poet for whom it was necessary relentlessly to pose the existential questions, makes mild fun of the human need to know the wherefore of all things in "Ormen" [The Worm, II:278–81]. A young couple watches a tiny green worm trying to make its way to the top of a blade of grass. To them it looks like a living question mark "that has fallen over and is walking on all fours" as it loops and inches its way forward. The lowly worm's purpose and place in the greater scheme of things becomes the fascinating question to these young lovers; but the worm itself neither seeks nor needs answers. It has courage, persistence, and time. Touched by the insect's brave, possibly meaningless struggle, the young lovers kiss, as if they had rediscovered something wonderful they had once known about each other. Six months later the husband gives his wife a sapphire question mark for Christmas.

"Hvepsen" [The Wasp, II:281–85] is similar in tone. Over a period of days an old man watches a dying wasp trying to reach what the man imagines to be its mate, already dead. He puzzles over the "story" behind the wasp's struggle toward reunion, but in the end all he can say is that the living wasp searched for its dead counterpart, reached it, and then lay down to die. Something in the insect's struggle—again, very likely its persistence in the face of meaninglessness—inspires the man's admiration for the normally despised wasps, prompting him to see their real beauty for the first time. But more importantly, the wasps have touched him so deeply that he reaches out in a gesture of love to his wife, something he has not done for a long time.

In "Housewife" [II:252–54] Obstfelder assumed the persona of a middle-aged woman who feels her youth slipping from her. The poem begins:

> —Housewife, four children.
> She has covered her face with her hands. She sees
> a white sail gliding slowly away. Her youth.
> —Housewife, four children.

The statement of her situation—"Housewife, four children"—structurally encloses the image of her covered face as her actual situation of wife and mother confines her now in an uneasy despair.

But then she opens a window—an apparent gesture toward freedom—and sees a yellow butterfly.[24] She seems to fear the butterfly, hiding from it behind the piano. But it finds her and lights on her hand; and her fear for herself becomes fear for the butterfly. She warns it, "I am soon an old woman. My room is too small for you." Concerned that it shall die, she carries it to the window and sets it free. It lands on "the eye of a wild rose," kisses it, and flies away. She notices that the rose is wet. The butterfly carried a tear she shed on its wing and left it with the rose. The tear—shed perhaps for her lost youth, or for the fragile life of the butterfly, or for life itself—seems to free her. Life quickens in her, she feels sensuous and beautiful, and she has a wonderful fantasy:

I want to put on my gold silk, and my arm will be naked. I'll put on my bridal shoes.
And when he comes, and when he asks:
—Why have you put on your gold silk? I will answer:
—Because my shoulders are finer than the butterfly's wings.
And when he asks:
—Why do you have wild roses in your hair? I will answer:
—So that they should not wither without having seen a man's eye.
And when he asks:
—Why is your arm naked?
I will answer:
—Because I am young. Because my blood beats in the veins of my arm.

She imagines he will ask her whether she is his today, and she will answer, "You do not possess me. You borrow me from the great life that gives birth to roses and butterflies." Roses and butterflies die quickly; but through her identification with them the woman ceases to fear life. Gaining a new sense of power, beauty, and sensuality, she seems to embrace her own mortality.

The Strange Perspective of the Flowers

"Hepatica" and "The Violet" are both written in the style of a Hans Christian Andersen fairytale, the narrator speaking as if he were engaged in a conspiracy with the wise children against the not-so-wise adults. "The Violet" begins, for example, "A violet stands in the field, thinking. You mustn't believe that violets can't think. Many people say, of course, that the flowers can't. But that is due to the fact that people only know what they see." And seeing—that is, seeing poetically—is precisely what these poems too are about. They illustrate the freshness of the unique perspective and the freedoms and also the limitations of the subjective one. As often in the verse poetry, Obstfelder chose a naive tone and point of view in order to see things with more innocent eyes. The commonplace is defamiliarized and in the process made strange and wonderful.

"Blåveis" [Hepatica, II:254], written early in 1893, is one of two Obstfelder poems—the other being "I See"—familiar to most Norwegians. In a most unusual way it makes a rare treasure of the common little flower so abundant in Norway in spring. The entire text follows:

> I stroll up the hills. The pure snow shoots
> out sparks.
> There comes a little girl. My, how she trudges along
> on her tiny legs!
> What has she got? Hepatica!
> Hepatica! So early. February, ski tracks, furry young ladies.
> My heavens, it is hepatica! And a great big bouquet
> at that.
> Here she comes. Nine years old. Curls.
> "What did you do with your hepatica?"
> "Hepatica! I have no hepatica."
> "Of course you do. I saw it with my own eyes. And
> a great big bouquet at that."
> But she *has* no hepatica bouquet.
> She just has two big child eyes, the little girl,
> just two eyes that smile and shine and shower stars of
> twinkling hepatica.

The poem is about the unusual or the magical vision that can see flowers in February in the eyes of a little girl. And these are such extraordinary flowers, too, for they are not simply flowers in the snow but the eyes of a little girl that never quite recede back into being just normal big blue child's eyes. The dynamic image of the hepatica eyes—flowers disappearing into the little girl's eyes which become once again twinkling flowers—brings a wonderful touch of madness to the poem. What the wanderer saw and did not see he sees once again.

"Violen" [The Violet, II:260–62] from the same period, is easily seen as an allegorical statement of Obstfelder's organic view of life. Its theme is the perception of one little violet contrasted with what less innocent observers with a larger perspective—we the readers—see. The object in question first appears in the violet's field (where it stands thinking, of course) as a "fine little foot in a little shiny shoe," but in no time we can guess just what this strange creature is. As the narrator says:

> You have probably already guessed that the foot wasn't strolling alone through the meadow. No, there was a leg above it, of course, and above the leg a waist, and above the waist a neck and above the neck a face with eyes in it and together they make a girl.

But from the violet's lowly perspective the creature looks quite different.

> —What is this white thing that is red at the same time with a stem and then another stem that is bigger and another big, big stem, and a stem with something yellow around it, and a stem that is smaller than the others but much, much thicker. Oh, the sun and the sky have quite disappeared, it's so dark. I think I'm going to die.

This tangle of strange stems is, of course, the girl's hand encircling the violet as she bends down to pick it.

Terrified but excited by its sudden separation from one field and its relocation on another—the girl's bosom—the sensitive little violet feels something akin to spiritual bliss. He experiences her thoughts as song, her spirit as the wind, and the rhythm of her breathing as the rhythm of the world. Again the violet thinks it might die, but from ecstasy now, not fear.

The violet is unable to anticipate what really happens in the end. The last thing it sees is the nearing of "the white stems and the blue suns." The girl bends her face down to the flower and a tear drop falls in its eye. The violet hastens to suck up the tear, thinking it will be like the morning dew. But it is hot and bitter and the violet folds its petals together in pain.

The poem can be interpreted as Obstfelder's world view in miniature. Reality is experienced as both fragmented and frightening, on the one hand, mysterious and wonderful on the other. The poet urgently hopes for a rhythmical unity behind it all, a unity that he, like the violet, is too small to see. He imagines a protective motherly haven in the cosmos but is also hurt by it, as the flower is hurt by the girl's tear.

These poems in particular are reminiscent of earlier poems like "Spring" and "Rain," Obstfelder showing that it is the perspective of a child or a flower or a rain drop or a mad wanderer that helps us to see something old as new, something ordinary as mysterious, something familiar as if for the first time.

The "Folktales"

A few of the prose poems closely resemble folktales, the major figures in all of them young women, some frightened, some sad, and all very innocent. The poems attempt primarily to capture their elusive moods as did the quartet "Girls," from 1890.

The most interesting and most experimental of these poems are two—from early 1893—conceived as texts to accompany paintings with folktale motifs done by the Norwegian painter Gerhard Munthe.[25] Both poems are written as dialogues between three sisters. In "De tre kongedøtre og den friske sang" [The Three Royal Daughters and the Fresh Song, II:257–59], the innocent sisters are lured from the safety of their quiet grove by a young knight who claims to be the fresh song they hear. "I sing of life's loveliness, I sing of the white, swelling sails, I sing of the joyful beating of my heart." But danger lurks outside the grove. A fox waits, perhaps the knight in disguise. A warning is issued in the refrain that continually interrupts

the sisters' dialogue, but they do not seem to hear. The poem ends as
the knight coaxes the young women out into the world.

—Come, follow my ship, noble ladies. Now the wind is good.

—Listen, the ocean roars, sisters!
—See, the sail swells, sisters!
—Oh come, come!

The fox caught three white deer.

The mood of the poem is anxious. Innocence is threatened.

In the second text, "Mørkræd" [Fear of the Dark, II:259–60],
the mood turns to angst. Three little sisters, left alone, try to calm
each other's fear of the dark. They imagine animal sounds in the
wind, a punishing God in the clouds, and terrible visions on the walls.
The final dialogue between them should be read in whispers.

—Oh, do you see something moving on the wall,
Elfrid?
—I see a head, Elfrid, I see horrid teeth. Oh
hold my hand!
—It's just the moon, Valborg.

—But something is screaming, Elfrid.
—Something's calling my name, Elfrid.
—It's just the wind, Gjertrud.

The one sister tries to comfort the other, but her reassuring words are
lost in the sinister wind.

The Myths of Creation

In a more somber mood Obstfelder wrote four poems reminiscent
of myths. Through these short, ambiguous tales he tells of a sad and
anxious creation. Its gods have fallen; their power is thwarted; they
themselves are imprisoned or exiled. He uses a variety of mystifying
techniques to make the tales seem simultaneously familiar and strange,
with the result that they read like myths heard once long ago and then
almost forgotten.

In "Av 'Eventyrarabesk' " [Folktale Arabesque, II:249–50] Obstfelder employs the familiar pattern of the fairytale, beginning the
poem, "Once upon a time there was a great and mighty king." As in
the traditional tale the king has three sons; but these sons, who loved
each other so much that they could never be parted, do not go seeking
their fortune, but rather their misfortune. In a faraway land there
lived a princess, "white and beautiful, but proud and cold." One day
she approached one of the sons and simply looked at him, "with her
eyes," as the poem says. He forgot everything, rushed toward her, and
looked into those powerful eyes. He died, but his soul lived on as the
ocean. The second brother went in search of the first, and when he
saw his body his heart broke and his soul became the sky. The third
brother went in search of the other two until he died of sorrow. His
soul became the forest that "wanders toward the ocean and is washed
by its tears, and the ocean wanders toward the sky without reaching
it." The poem ends:

> But the sun was the king, and the moon was the princess,
> and when the spell is broken, then all the souls of the
> earth will be gathered together, then all the bells of
> the earth will ring.

The major theme of the tale is one that Obstfelder wrote about in
the poetry of 1890, i.e., a creation sighing for release. The world,
born out of evil, sorrow, and searching, longs for the bad spell to be
broken and harmony to be restored, here in the bonds of sibling love.
The prediction in the last sentence that this will one day come about
enhances the present tension of this world held in sorrowful suspension,
the sea wandering forever toward the sky.

A secondary theme is the "great and mighty" king's lack of
omnipotence. He only owns "almost" everything and he only knows
"almost" everything. Implicit in the tale is the idea that he did not
have the power to save his sons nor is he able to recover them, existing
in a state of abeyance with the wicked princess moon. The powerlessness of the father/god will be a more predominant theme in the poems
that follow.

In "Fairytale Arabesque" Obstfelder provides us with an apparent referent—the fairytale pattern of the king and his sons—and then alters it slightly, giving us the impression that we know the tale. This enables him, too, to refer to things within the poem as if they had known symbolic value. For example, the princess's fatal eyes are treated as an obvious and well-known danger. Staring into a woman's eyes often means death in Obstfelder's poetic universe, but it is not an immediately recognized symbol. Yet here it is used as if it were part of the stock of traditional folklore symbols. In various ways the poem pretends to have a universality that it actually does not have but which it paradoxically then assumes.

"Jeg'et" [The I, II:270-71], from the fall of 1894, is a second poem about creation, but its structure is more open and its meaning more ambiguous than the fairytale. The narrator, the "I" of the title, is the creator of the world.

> I drew the water's broad, peaceful line. . . .
> I let the green earth bend down on both sides of the
> fjord and drink the water. It has laced its edge with
> leaves and evergreen branches and slowly waving flowers.
> And beneath the leaves men and women walk in
> flocks and pairs. I have tuned the air, the leaves, the
> water, I have built mankind's ear in rich harmony.
> I walk alone among them and listen to them laugh to
> each other and whisper the words of love.

But the god grows restless in his creation. Inexplicably it becomes foreign to him and he leaves. Failure to provide motive is one of the most important mystifying techniques used in the poem. It creates a sense of uncertainty, encouraging us to supply possible explanations. Where does the cause of the god's alienation lie? in himself? or in the world he has created? Is he alone among men? Does his creation disappoint him? or does it reject him?

For whatever reason, he leaves behind him the sounds of laughter and song, slowly climbing toward the mountains. In his retreat he can hear only the whispering heather and the sighing of the glacier. And he expresses a longing for someone, apparently like himself, to come and marvel and admire and say:

> I saw the sea and the sky and the haze of colors and the
> wonder of man. And I grew more and more alone. Because I
> longed to know the one whose imagination created sea and
> clouds, whose thought built the ear of man.

The poem ends here, the god longing for one curious man with no reassurance that the man is even interested in this god who has slowly walked away from his creation.

Any number of interpretations are possible. The poem may be an explanation of the lack of spirituality in a world abandoned by god, or it may be a tale of the god's own helplessness, imprisoned behind the glaciers and the whispering heather. On the other hand, it may intend to explain *man's* everpresent longing for something harmonious and complete. It may also be, as Hannevik suggested, "the poet's imagination that is spoken of here or it might be such, from an idealistic world view, that it is the subject creating himself in his own world."[26] Whatever the interpretation, the final impression is of a lonely creator, powerless to make man come to him.

A more urgent picture of the powerless god is "Fangen" [The Prisoner, II:237].[27] The entire poem follows.

> In the center of the earth is a cell. On its
> wet floor lies a prisoner staring out into the darkness
> with glowing eyes. His limbs are bones, his face a
> skull, because for thousands of years no man's voice has
> echoed in his ear, no woman's hand stroked his burning
> forehead.
>   Sometimes his chains shake as if in pain or rage.
> Then the prisons of all lands totter, and the just of the
> earth run to defend and secure them.
>   Men are the masters of the earth. In its center
> lies earth's god, chained and in darkness, listening,
> listening.
>   Will the prisons fall soon?

The central image of the poem is simple and stark, the skeleton god lying imprisoned in his own creation. But typically the poem inspires more questions than it provides explanations. The god is chained, but will he one day break loose? He lies listening for something. Is it for help from a fellow prisoner/god on earth? for the nearing of a man's voice or a woman's hand? Who imprisoned the god? his own people? or are they unaware of his presence in the middle of their world? Man's prisons are somehow connected with the god's. How? Does mankind imprison its saints as it seems to have its god? Will the god be able to break free? Even the narrator does not seem to know.

The skeleton god becomes an eerie metaphor for the thwarted state of creation. But, as in "The I," the powerless god may also refer to the poet or the creative self. Obstfelder often used the image of the poet in the cell to convey his feelings of spiritual and psychological confinement.

The last poem,"Pilen" [The Arrow, II:250–51], from the late summer of 1892, is the most obscure of all the "myths." The major motif is once again the uncertainty of god's power, here portrayed as random, ineffectual, and ultimately destructive. The poem begins with the image of a radiant hand stretching out into space. "A white hand hangs suspended in space, a radiant hand. Lightening shoots from its finger tips. It stretches out, and worlds lie in darkness, and thousand year old tribes dance the dance of death." Above the dark shadows of the dancers rise the white backs of the flagellants. When he with "the whitest hand" sees them he cuts his hand, drawing a drop of innocent blood. And he takes an arrow from his six thousand year old quiver, dips it in his blood, and aims at the flagellants. But the arrow flies past them and falls among those who are "dancing life's dance in the dark." They die immediately, for "the divine blood is poison on earth." And the poem ends: "The white backs wander on, in lonely majesty. Are the powers of heaven challenged from the shadow realms?"

The poem is based on a series of major and minor ironies. The one who has the whitest hand is probably meant to be the creator of the world, and the dancers, the living. The flagellants oppose the god and his dancers in some unclear way. Most likely they are the oppressors of the joy of life. Though they seem to oppose the god, however, they do no direct harm to the dancers. It is, in fact, the god who brings darkness and death into the dancers' world when he stretches out his hand; and it is he who destroys them in an apparent effort to destroy their enemy. The ironies exist on all levels. The god is of innocent blood and good intentions, but he brings destruction. The flagellants ravage themselves but go on living. Strangely, the god and the flagellants share the same white radiance, while the dancers dance in darkness. The opposition in the poem is between the forces of life and death, but it is totally unclear to whom the forces belong. They seem partially invested in each, the god, the dancers, and the flagellants. But the only definitive conclusions are that the dancers are powerless for they depend on the white hand of the god, and the god's power can be thwarted so that he destroys his own, leaving him powerless himself in some other unknown hand.

Taken together, these prose poems present a picture of an impotent father/god. Compared to most of Obstfelder's poetry and prose, there is a conspicuous absence of the powerful feminine presence in the self and the universe. In this group of poems the force at the center is clearly masculine, but it is wounded and helpless.

Chapter Five

The Prose

The "I-Form"

Obstfelder's earliest writings had been short pieces of prose, biographical and fictional sketches, tales, travelogues, and stories. Throughout his life he continued to work with prose, even during the most prolific of the poetry years; in spite of the fact that he is remembered as a poet, prose seemed to come most naturally to him. He brought poetic language closer to prose, and he truly excelled at the prose poem. It was therefore only a matter of time before he began to experiment with longer fiction.

Between the fall of 1893 and the summer of 1896 he wrote and published two short stories, "Liv" and "Sletten" [The Plain], and a longer novella, *Korset* [The Cross]. At his death he was working on his most ambitious project, the diary novel *En prests dagbog* [A Cleric's Journal], published posthumously. (The *Journal* will be discussed separately in chapter 7 due to its place and importance in Obstfelder's work.) He also wrote shorter pieces of prose, too long to be considered prose poems yet too losely structured to be short stories. Two of them, "Den ubekjendte" [The Unknown One] and "Høst" [Autumn] are treated here to add nuance to the picture of the prose.

For in a way, Obstfelder wrote the same strange love story—with variations—again and again. All three stories involve similar haunted lovers, the irremediably lonely seeker and his beautiful soul-mate. Their story is an 1890s cliché. The young man, yearning to experience life's essence, has withdrawn from the community into the peace and isolation of his own soul; but he "accidentally" encounters a young woman, herself set apart from society in some way, and a mysterious, mood-filled relationship develops between them. Through his love for the woman the man experiences life more profoundly than ever before. She, however, dies or undergoes a death ritual in order that the poet might live.

Erotic love appears to play a more significant and succoring role, not in "Liv," but in the later works, "The Plain" and *The Cross*. For the first time in Obstfelder's writing the man's love for the woman is made richer and more human, encompassing feelings of an emotional, spiritual, and physical nature which complement rather than contradict each other. Arne Hannevik considered the apparent acceptance of erotic love a major and mature change in Obstfelder's work.[1] But whether erotic love is so fully integrated into Obstfelder's and the protagonist's perspectives is a matter of interpretation. And contradictions abound. The physical love relationship, though accepted, is never actually described. In "The Plain" the erotic bond functions most importantly as a metaphor for spiritual communion between man and God. The man's love for the woman in *The Cross* leads him to insane jealousy from which he finds no peace until she is dead. Only then does he have his epiphany.

None of these is really a true love story, except in the most narcissistic sense, for they are all essentially concerned with one person, the poetic seeker. He is the protagonist, the narrator, and the sole determiner of reality in the story. All characters and all events exist only relative to him. He sees himself in everything and everyone, and thus all things, particularly the woman, become a reflection, an extension, a metaphor, or a distortion of himself.

There is no epic development, little tension, and virtually no action in these stories, the weak story line barely able to support a fictional structure at all. What little action takes place is generally told after the fact, the course of events being at all times secondary to sounding the emotional and spiritual depths of the protagonist. His character emerges not through personal *bildung* and dramatic encounters but through a mosaic of moods, reflections, reminiscences, projections, and ponderings, inspired most often by the woman fate strangely arranged for him to meet.

Like much of the poetry, the stories employ the fugue-like structure, themes introduced and then brought back in variation in order to bring out the overtones and undertones of the protagonist's personality.

Obstfelder felt strongly about this particular fictional form. He was not given to polemical writing, but twice he felt it necessary to speak up publicly as a writer. The first time, in the middle of the decade, had been to praise and thank the generation of writers who preceded him, the so-called Realists/Naturalists, under attack for immoralities of all kinds. Although not one of them, he felt obliged to defend them. But the second and last time he felt he had to speak out, he did so in defense of the genre he considered his own.

The article "Jeg-formen i litteraturen" [The I-Form in Literature], written just before he died and published, as Obstfelder left it, three weeks later,[2] was a defense of first-person narrative against prominent critic Edvard Brandes's accusation that it was confessional and easy. Obstfelder's contrary belief that first-person narration was artistically sophisticated, sound, and rich in possibilities inspired the article which has become an informal manifesto. It reads in part:

> Dr. Edvard Brandes writes a sentence that seems to me unworthy of a man of *his* sensitivity. It is a kind of word game: If only the I-form didn't exist, if only these people could keep their *I* out of their books!
>
> Herr Edv. Brandes knows full well that the pronoun doesn't decide it, *he* is more often a transposed I, a false *he*, than the I is the author's *I*. . . . The I-form is born of the need to go right to the bottom of that person or the specific state of mind one imagines. . . . No form demands such keen hearing. The he-form covers up, one can fill it up as one can a sack, with one's own personality, with what one has seen, with what one poeticizes—The I-form needs absolute metallic clarity, no alloying is tolerated. . . .
>
> The I-form is also a result of the need to go deeper. The drama presents characters through their external reflections, the novel combines, spins together persons, events. The I-form wants to reach what is between and behind all this. For that matter it is a monologue. But it is more.
>
> It is an independent art form. (III:306–307)

Through this form Obstfelder could explore at length the "I" or the self familiar from the poetry. He is supremely sensitive, registering the slightest fluctuation in mood, the slightest change in nature, intuiting correspondences among himself, others, and the world, at brief moments penetrating life's mysterious, metaphysical dimension.

But the I-narrator was much more than a sophisticated literary device to Obstfelder. He clearly intended close identification among author, narrator/protagonist, and sympathetic reader. Together they would explore the depths of one fictional soul, and in the process reach into themselves and out to each other. Intense communication between poet and reader was possible, Obstfelder believed, through the "I-form."

The I-form has the ability to create an echo like no other form of pure poetry. . . . It emanates from a vision like a pure hallucination, and it would be strange if its intensity at times did not cause others to tremble and listen, listen for what the poet wants to say. Because the poet, like every artist, is not interested in the work itself but in the infinitely greater, deeper, more beautiful dimension that the work calls forth. (III:308)

The I-narrator was intended to be a sort of metaphysical medium through whom "poet" and reader communicated their deepest feelings.

But in reality he functions as much as a negative as a positive force both on his surroundings and the reader. Like the haunted child of the poetry, he is a passive man. The woman, typically, is the active partner. He often speaks in a monotone and is totally uninterested in the normal course of events. And although he is intensely sensitive to life, he too is equally drawn toward death, finding in death's presence life's supreme moment. He can thus have a nearly paralyzing effect on the objects, both human and nonhuman, that he brings into his frame of reference.

The narrator's very personality seems to work against Obstfelder's intent. But the problem was not specific to him. The Danish/American critic, Niels Ingwersen, has characterized the nonepic prose of the Scandinavian 1890s in this way:

The fragile plot line ties together a series of descriptive states, but on the whole action and experience fade in favor of mood appreciation, reflection, lyrical moments, dreams (at times hallucinations) and memory. The protagonist projects his own moods on the surroundings which thereby lose their own value and become symbols. . . . Reflections on existence are frequent and manifold, but they lack energy and direction. The protagonist seems to get closer to himself when he indulges in lyrical dreams and unbinding fantasies.[3]

To Ingwersen the unepic form is both symptomatic and metaphoric of this pessimistic and fatalistic decade, expressing "profound doubt about the ability of the individual to change his or her fate."[4] In place of

philosophy, ideology, or belief—the foundations of an epic structure—
the 1890s writers substituted the self, their exquisite refuge; but it
proved inadequate. "Worship of the self, which seems to have been a
last resort, does not lead to any uplifting experience of the riches of
the self, rather to a helpless awareness of its poverty."[5]

Although Ingwersen's conclusion must be cautiously applied to
Obstfelder—who never ceased to believe in the "riches of the self"—
it does speak directly to the problematic nature of these stories which
at the same time profess a positive and a deeply pessimistic view of
life.

And indeed it may be that Obstfelder, though he never grew cynical
toward the narrator-self, grew nevertheless more and more skeptical of
him. There seems to be evidence for this if we take seriously the slight
technical changes in point of view from the first story to the last,
changes which serve increasingly to expose the narrator as a potentially
destructive force. In "Liv," narrator and implied narrator are essentially one, the protagonist being the most sensitive character and an
absolutely innocent one. In "The Plain" there seems to be a
momentary split between implied narrator and the protagonist, whose
sensitivity is seen as possibly harmful to life. In *The Cross* Obstfelder
deliberately sought to achieve distance between the two "voices," the
narrator putting himself on trial, if only to determine he had "acted"
properly. In each story the narrator/protagonist *is* found innocent and
redeemed. But if narrative technique can be taken as an indication,
Obstfelder grew increasingly suspicious of the sensitive poet, looking
for more sophisticated ways of revealing his destructive side. Interestingly, *A Cleric's Journal* is told through a schizophrenic minister. As
in the poetry, Obstfelder may have needed two voices, and particularly
the voices of extremes, in order to tell his story.

"Liv"

Obstfelder wrote "Liv" (II:3–20)[6] in Copenhagen in the fall of
1893,[7] at the same time as he wrote the darkest of the prose poems. In
contrast to the poems, this gentle story is a hymn to life, albeit a
decadent hymn, praising life sighing and dying and struggling to be
born. The story takes its name from Liv—which means "life" in
Norwegian—the young woman dying of consumption. In the dying

virgin Obstfelder found an ideal symbol through which his protagonist might view himself and life in a mysterious and delicate light. Like the bride of the poem "The Bride's Pale Face," she is poised on the brink of her initiation into life. At this moment in time she is most receptive: open, vulnerable, sensitive, and emotionally taut. The irony that she is dying before she should experience life is a cruel but all the more meaningful truth to Obstfelder and his protagonist. In the face of her own death she is most keenly aware of life's possibilities. Yet at the same time she can only know them as possibilities, as longings, dreams, and fantasies, not realities, and she therefore remains untouched and undisappointed. Through her the narrator/poet enters a world of greater purity, mystery, and nuance than this one, a world— it will be seen—of beautiful reflections of Liv and himself.

He is a man who has shunned society even before he meets Liv. He opens his story with a description of the street in which he lives. Tenant and landscape are obviously one, the street a metaphorical extension of himself.

A large city has dim corners, side streets with mysterious names, names which provoke awareness of life's dusk, where much happens that even books don't know.

I live at the moment in such a street. It is so quiet there. A milk wagon might drive by, or a coal cart, or a grinder might walk from house to house. But afterwards it is doubly quiet here. (3)

Through the lonely city landscape the poet reveals the mood of his own soul. And like the street, so every person and every object will exist only relative to him. Everything serves him as a mirror.

He prefers to remain within the protective confines of the extraordinary, having withdrawn from normal life and ordinary people. He found them bothersome at best, profane at worst, and now chooses the peace and solitude of his secret street.

His withdrawal must be interpreted on one level as the persistent desire of Obstfelder's narrator to remain a child. He has left behind a world captured for him in the memory of a woman he once knew, a woman full of life, love, health, and vigor.

It seems so far away. Her red, happy cheeks, the laughter in her eyes bursting with desire to hop right out into life, whatever it was, whether it brought joy or sorrow,—the blond nights at home,—it's all become so mysteriously strange. (7)

Psychologically, his preference for the tubercular child must be seen as a wish to remain free of the responsibilities, sexual and otherwise, of the adult. At the same time, however, he is able to channel his sexual feelings through the metaphor of her disease.

This was, of course, a common phenomenon in the art of the 1890s. In *Illness as Metaphor* Susan Sontag wrote regarding the use of the tubercular victim by the artists of the late nineteenth century:

Like all really successful metaphors, the metaphor of TB was rich enough to provide for two contradictory applications. It described the death of someone (like a child) thought to be too "good" to be sexual, the assertion of an angelic psychology. It was also a way of describing sexual feelings—while lifting the responsibility for libertinism which is blamed on a state of objective, physiological decadence or deliquescence.[8]

Obstfelder's narrator often uses sexual imagery to describe nature, spiritual imagery to describe Liv. What he must repress in terms of the woman he has chosen to love, he transfers to a completely unthreatening phenomenon, i.e., nature.

The only thing of the outside world that interests him is the unseen woman who lives above him. He listens carefully to the sounds of her footsteps, and as her routine becomes familiar to him, she becomes an object not only of fascination but of real concern. He worries that she might be lonely, and *he* feels lonely when she goes to bed and jealous when he thinks she has been with someone. He imagines her pale and alone, with thoughtful eyes and fine hands, and joys, longings, and sorrows to match his own.

But suddenly one day he no longer hears her and distress forces him to her room. Their initial meeting—as if best communicated by silence—is not narrated. But he tells his readers that her name is Liv and she is exactly as he imagined her to be. What he had not anticipated was that she is dying.

Like the narrator, Liv is set apart from life; though he has chosen his isolation, she has not. She is not only ill but completely alone, with no parents, no friends, and far away from home. She comes originally from Iceland—the island of ice—a landscape as befitting her as the city streets the narrator.

But though lonely and dying, Liv brings renewed life to the narrator. Withdrawing even more completely from the outside world to watch over her, he grows daily in her innocent likeness. "Something pure and chaste has come over me. Liv's thoughts. They fold themselves around me like a white garment" (11). And he, too, brings life to Liv, telling her of the things she will never know or experience. Sharing their longings, their dreams and their sadness, the two come together in a union not of this world, he, in fact, growing more and more a stranger in the world of the living, though he is reawakening to life itself.

As she is dying Liv has a fantasy of Iceland washed by warmer waters over time. "The screes and glaciers are gone and thick, shaggy forests keep you warm and keep out the wind and frost"(17). Her fantasy of the two lovers on the "tropical" island symbolizes the momentary transformation her innocence and warmth have wrought in the narrator.

After her death he is more alone than before. Life seems to him a prostitution of his beloved, and once again the city street becomes a projection of his mood. Interestingly, he chooses sexual imagery to describe his disgust.

The boulevards make me sick. The curving breasts, the uplifted heads, the costumes that sway on lovely lithe hips, the smiles—all this that cries: kiss, live, enjoy,—women lifted by loving man's hands into closed, dark carriages, sounds of kisses behind doors, sounds of toasting with bad wine, clammy handshakes of fawning friends— —oh it's so nauseating. (19)

He feels he must get farther and farther away from the city. There is something he must find out although what it is is unclear. Typically for Obstfelder's protagonist, he ends his story with a question. "When all the grating noise is silenced, when I am forgotten and when I myself have forgotten, will it then come, and everything become clear, and my soul awaken?" (20). At least partially the answers lay in the mystery of Liv, apparently no longer accessible to him. But in the course of the story a curious thing has occurred. Everything has become a reflection of everything else: the city landscape of the narrator, Iceland of Liv, Liv of the narrator, the narrator of Liv, and, of course, Liv of that innocent, mysterious life the narrator so longingly seeks. Although he has lost her to death, her image is imprinted in his memories, his projections, and his symbols, i.e., in himself.

More than a love story, "Liv" is a story of spiritual rebirth. Through the woman's dying the narrator is reborn, as if he vicariously descends into hell in order to reach heaven. The ritualistic pattern underlying "Liv" is also central in "The Plain" and *The Cross*.

"Autumn"

"Liv" is a joyous tale in a spiritual sense, but the fatalism of the decade is its underlying attitude. The self, paradoxically, is the sole determiner of reality and yet helpless to control its destiny. The only form of control is to yield to the fateful forces of life, and thus the narrator is, to use Hannevik's expression, "consciously passive" in order to remain receptive.[9]

The theme of submission to the forces of life (and death) is common in Obstfelder's work, particularly in early poems such as "All Creation Sighs" and "Tempest." The most haunting illustration of the theme in the prose is the short sketch entitled "Høst" [Autumn, III:72–77], probably written in the winter of 1894–1895.[10] Unlike the other prose, it is not written in the guise of a love story, but it is an insightful introduction into the character of the passive lovers. Any one of them could have known and learned from this strange man born of autumn.

The sketch is as subdued and slow-moving as the poem "Tempest" is frenetic. The narrator—about whom little is known except that he seems to live by himself in a lonely heathlike landscape—tells of a mysterious man who occasionally comes to visit on stormy fall evenings. Barely separable from the heath, the man is the incarnation of this season of beauty and death, brutally powerful, yet gentle at the same time.

He is tall. His strong arms hang as if he were ashamed of their power and would prefer to deny it. He walks with slightly stooped shoulders. (73)

. . . an impassive pride rests on his long, narrow face with its pointed beard, but with his first words the pride melts into something womanly tender. It is as if a woman has taken her place inside him and remade him in her image. (75)

This androgynous, autumnal man brings peace to the narrator through his presence and his insight into the natural world. Before his arrival the narrator had been musing over the tragic, doomed battle the heath must fight against the destruction of the season. So sure that all life resists death, inevitable though it may be, he imagined autumn to be an unwilling man with a sorrowful face, forced against his will to walk the heath at night in rhythm with the rain, stepping on each blade of grass and picking every leaf.

But the true autumn man teaches him otherwise. Nature understands dying. It *wants* to die.

. . . nature has its loveliest life when it pales. Nothing dies as beautifully as leaves. They dress themselves in the warmest, most beautiful colors the earth possesses. They embrace death, longing to feel the delicate change that will take place in them. (75)

Death comes to the leaves like a gentle, sensual lover.

The narrator listens as if he were in the presence of a prophet. Human beings, the autumnal man teaches, must learn from nature how to die, how to embrace the inevitable life forces, not to fight them. And indeed it seems as if all the protagonists of the love stories have sat at the wise man's feet. They are passive, yet receptive. They long for life, yet hanker for death like the leaves in fall. And all go through the same ritual, symbolically passing through the doors of death, thereby gaining a heightened awareness of life.

"The Plain"

Early in 1895 Obstfelder wrote to a friend that although he thought he had found a simple prose form in "Liv" it now no longer satisfied him. He was searching for something "stronger and with more life content."[11] "The Plain" (II:21–39) was the result.[12] He wrote and rewrote the story in the first part of 1895, moving from Stockholm to Copenhagen to Berlin. He was unusually enthusiastic about "The Plain," describing it in a letter as "the most beautiful and stylistically the best" he had ever done.[13]

More notable, however, than any significant change in style is an apparent change in the protagonist, who embraces a more affirming view of life, symbolized in his union with the woman, Naomi. They enter into a relationship in which the spiritual bond is primary but not to the exclusion of earthly ties. Hannevik considered the change in the protagonist to be crucial in Obstfelder's work. "Liv" and "Autumn," he said, "were both about searching spirits who, out of a strong, religious need to know were driven farther and farther from a normal way of life. . . . They found no answers." But in "The Plain" and the later novella, *The Cross*, "it seems that the relationship to a woman offers a 'resolution' to these questions."[14] The marriage on the mountain plain is certainly intended to symbolize a triumph of love and life over death, and in that sense there is resolution and even liberation.

But there is a discrepancy in "The Plain" between form and content. Like "Liv," it is pregnant with death imagery, its optimism at best paradoxical. The protagonist affirms life, but he is really a creature of the darkness, drawing Naomi into it with him. And she, although a symbolic wife, remains like Liv a reflection of him.

The significant difference between "Liv" and "The Plain" lies not so much in style or underlying attitude but in the complexity of the protagonist. The narrator of "Liv" is meant to be emotionally and spiritually superior to everyone, including Liv and the reader, and he is meant to be accepted as absolutely sincere. The narrator of "The Plain" is both a more complicated and a more human man. He has a greater range of emotions and is prey to more fears, ambivalences, and minor deceits. Essentially the same type—the sensitive poet—he is seemingly viewed with greater objectivity. His sensitivity is not only his greatest strength but also his greatest weakness. His rejection of society is treated as symptomatic of both his advanced spiritual state and his frightened social persona. And he proves to be naive about his own motivations. Although this poet-narrator, like that of "Liv," will ultimately be rewarded for his sensitivity, he is viewed here as potentially harmful to himself and to others, the ambiguous portrayal undoubtedly the result of Obstfelder's own unresolved ambivalence.

The narrator is anonymous, save for his thirty-four years. He is afraid he will now never discover "life's loveliness" (37), his expression for life lived in sensitive and strong communion with nature and with God. He has left the city, the landscape of "Liv," because "Everything is so split, so small" (22), and has sought out a landscape quite different, the mountain plain, similar to the open, haunted heath of "Autumn." ("The Plain" was probably the inspiration for "Autumn.")[15] In "Liv" the narrator projects himself into images with a definite form: the black and white city street, the pale virgin, the attic room, the island of Iceland. These isolated, contained images mirror the poet's personal isolation and containment. The mountain plain, in comparison, is open and without bounds, a land in which the poet feels life expanding rather than contracting. He loves its many moods, in all of them sensing liberation of the spirit. Its light brings him hope, inspiration, and wisdom. But like the autumnal man he finds the darkness even richer and more alluring than the light. "It is an ocean in which you always imagine something is happening, roots creep and life crawls and fates wind,—outward, not pent up, outward toward the next morning" (22).

Such love of the darkness is ominous. His story takes place when "summer expires," when "the green has begun to burst into innumerable sparks that flush toward death" (30). The plain, lonely and hushed, is far from the crowd of the living; and its expansiveness can exhilarate, but it can also terrify.

The plain is so boundless. So much that is unknown lives over the endless ranges of vision. The eye never finds rest. It runs and runs over grass and rocks, it gets nowhere, it finds only the unfathomable darkness and high above, the threatening stars, and, behind them, the blue abyss, the most terrifying of all. (31–32)

Like the feminine cosmos of "Without Name," "Eve," and "Barcarole," the plain is a land of death in life. The poet/narrator, looking for a life more perfect and pure than reality, steps into the Symbolists' land of symbols and dreams, where the dividing line between life and death is blurred.

Very early in his narrative he says, "Something in this light and the muted sound of the plain melts together with your dreams" (21). Indeed, he tells his story as if he were speaking from a dream. His language is soft and muted. As in the distorted world of dreams, everything can be an event, a meeting, a single word, a silence, and to every event can be attributed equal import. He speaks of a great range of emotions—joy, alienation, fear, sadness—but since he filters everything through his brooding, dreamer's eye all expressions of emotion, whether of joy or sorrow, are exquisitely sensitive but nearly indistinguishable, the one from the other.

The narrator's sensitivity is both his blessing and his curse. It brings him closer to the pulse and poetry of life, leads him inexplicably to Naomi, and enables him to see what very few ever see. But it also cripples him. The greatest difference between the narrator of Liv and this one is the awareness that so much sensitivity and introspection can make a man emotionally unfit. "You walk with angst for life and angst for death, you don't dare tread heavily for fear of killing buds, you don't dare hum for fear of waking sleeping butterflies, you walk with the fear of death inside . . ." (24).

"The Plain" is structured as a series of strange trysts between the narrator and Naomi, the woman through whom his crippling fear is healed. They first meet at a party, then in his room, at a dance, and finally on the eerie plain. They utter very few words, overwhelmed by each other's presence and communicating on such a deep level that talk is unnecessary.

Like Liv, Naomi is a woman set apart. Whereas Liv is pale and dying, however, Naomi is aglow with life. She is the reddest flower, the brightest jewel, the fairest and the gayest at the ball. "For the first time I saw her together with other men. She glowed. She was as red as a fuschia" (32).

The lively Naomi and the introspective narrator are mysteriously, almost telepathically drawn to each other, as if they had long ago been party to the same dark secret. Behind the bloom of her cheeks, somewhere deep in the darkness of her eyes, the narrator senses a long forgotten fear. He cannot express it, but it seems to be the fear of death. "Her face lay white in front of me, her eyes looked at me a moment, large eyes—I only had the feeling of something large, dark, of something I once had seen in a dream long ago,—a second, then she lowered them" (28).

Together Naomi and the narrator exorcise their common fear through what can be interpreted as a sophisticated mental ritual, Naomi functioning as the medium of the exorcism. As she awakens the dark memory in the narrator, he awakens in her a painful awareness of death, as if drawing out of her his own fear. Their crucial meeting takes place at the dance. Naomi, a vision of swishing black silk, flowers, and glittering green jewels, is apparently oblivious to the narrator who stands watching her from afar. He then leaves, partly because he feels excluded from her circle, partly because a sense of death descends upon him and through him, upon her. But a terrified Naomi also leaves the dance and comes running toward him. Suddenly, she says,

I thought everything twirled and whirled, whirled purposelessly around, I thought all the faces were cowed, and all the words were screams and howls. The music began to ring in my ears: Someday you shall be dead, someday you shall be dead, someday you shall be dead. (34)

It is the image of the dance of death that now further binds the two. Although the narrator does not see Naomi for a period of time after the dance, he begins to connect her with the hitherto repressed death memory, pushing its way upward into consciousness. He anguishes over why she has brought it all back, and in this mood has a waking nightmare of her.

In the middle of the plain I see a house with shining eyes. A waltz sighs in the storm, shadows streak by the windows. There is a living being among them, her neck's white down glistens in the darkness, the black silk blazes, a crown of myrtle winds round her forehead, but her eyes are closed like those of a corpse. (35)

He becomes obsessed with the idea that he must rescue her from the dance of death, at the same time as he lives in terror that she is already dead.

Naomi then comes to him on the plain, more an apparition than a human being. She is changed. She is pale and no longer happy. She no longer loves to dance, but has withdrawn into her room, where she cries continuously because, she says, he has made her aware of how small she is and how large life. Filled with terror, she comes to him as there is no one else. In this eerie union of two people closer to death than to life, the poet discovers "life's loveliness" (37).

The final scene is of the narrator watching over his sleeping Naomi. They have been together five months and intend to remain on the mountain plain forever. It has become the protective, soothing mother-figure Obstfelder narrators continually seek out. ". . . the plain like an ocean rocked us to sleep. . . . Nowhere does nature draw these peaceful, long breaths as here" (38). In this protective environment the poet/narrator has been healed. "It no longer pains me, it is no longer strange and incomprehensible . . . there is a miracle in every raindrop" (38). But Naomi is the greatest miracle, for sometimes he can see the whole world behind her eyes. The story ends with the poet looking at the sleeping woman, a manifestation of Obstfelder's mother goddess, her face swimming in waves of hair, her breast heaving in rhythm with life itself. In her presence, he says, he senses the presence of God.

Thus Naomi and the narrator seemingly triumph over death. But there are too many contradictions. All gaiety, independence, and youth are wrung from Naomi as she is drawn into the poet's mental dance of death and purified of her profane existence in order to serve as his link to another life. Far more than his friend and lover, she has become a vehicle for his epiphany. The plain, reminiscent of the cosmic landscapes of amorphous gray and unending night, is a land of death, a land of silence and sleep, of passivity and pure self where the poet remains a child.

The Cross

The Cross (II:41–119) was written in the summer and published in the fall of 1896.[16] Although the longest of the love stories, it caused Obstfelder the least difficulty. Living in Paris and Copenhagen, he spent a lonely but rewarding summer. It was a time of inspiration, work, and freedom from self-doubt such as he seldom experienced. In a letter to the Danish critic Georg Brandes, asking him to read *The Cross,* he spoke as if he were for once in the hands of kinder fates. "So I have experienced this joyful, strangely delightful feeling that is part of being an artist,—in the last year it has worked its way up as if in crescendo and welled forth from all directions. . . ."[17]

Reaction to *The Cross* was and is mixed. Obstfelder considered it to be an "improvement" over earlier works, but he anticipated that Brandes might find it "more than permissably sentimental."[18] Brandes did not, however, and gave it a good review. Among Norwegians it is Obstfelder's most popular longer work, probably because it is his most accessible. Yet Hannevik considered it ordinary and unoriginal.[19]

But precisely in its ordinariness lies its extraordinary position in the context of Obstfelder's prose works. For the first time he focused directly on the dynamics of the love relationship, and in so doing critically examined the personality of the aesthetic narrator. In "The Plain" he suggested the destructive side of the neurasthenic artist. In *The Cross* he seemed to feel the need to go even further, exposing his narrator's possessiveness, egocentrism, and cruelty in relation to the woman he loved. There is even a question of whether he is a "murderer." To a limited extent the novella may be said to be an exposé of the aesthete.

But "limited extent" must be stressed, for at the conclusion of *The Cross* the narrator rests assured that he could not have been or have acted otherwise and that paradoxically his actions have brought both him and Rebekka closer to eternity. Essentially Obstfelder affirms his faith in his mystical fatalism.

And so perhaps after all life and that which comes to us from the outside exist only to be like a curved mirror, on which our insides roll forth in a many-sided, capriciously bent spiral until we have seen even the most distant, most hidden corner of ourselves. (116–17)

As in "Liv" and "The Plain" Obstfelder seems ambivalent to his material; and his attitude grows increasingly difficult to interpret. He may indeed have felt a greater and greater need to put the poet/child on trial. Given his own recurring self-hatred and self-doubt, this only seems likely. Equally possible is the idea that the guilty narrator made a far more interesting character than the spiritually innocent one. And still, by confirming the narrator's lack of guilt at the end of the story, Obstfelder essentially secured for himself the best of both worlds, the poet as the innocent child and as the demonridden man. The troubled protagonist also made possible more sophisticated experimentation in narrative technique, specifically in terms of the self-conscious, unreliable narrator so important in *The Cross*. It is, of course, impossible retrospectively to determine Obstfelder's motivation, but one thing remains a constant and that is the ambivalence itself.

The Cross is the narrator's account of his love affair with Rebekka. Writing frantically through all of one night as the memories of their months together rush in upon him, he seems to be in a race against the rising sun, needing to finish his story if he is to gain peace.

The narrator only gradually reveals the cause of his agitation. Several years ago Rebekka took her own life, ending their brief but intense love affair. Although she left a letter absolving him of all blame, he is still deeply troubled, unsure of the extent of his guilt. As if terrified of the truth, he initially conceals as much as he reveals. His deception concerns both the reader and himself, but as the story unfolds it becomes clear that on some level of consciousness he knows what he is doing. For example, he claims that he "has no time to shape [his] narrative artistically" (50), leading the reader to believe no structure exists. But most certainly one does. He begins with various portraits of Rebekka as a helpless and profoundly sad child who finds release, peace, and comfort in his arms, as if she were the child and he the mother.

> I don't know where the feeling came from. I often thought that a *heavy* burden lay upon my breast, that holding her while she cried was like a mother giving birth to a new human being. I thought I did something so deep and serious that it would be counted in my life's book. (45)

Only after portraying himself as Rebekka's comforter does he reveal that he is writing their story to gain peace of mind, and he withholds the fact that she has committed suicide, confessing his fear that he is the one "who perhaps drove her into death" (102) only after finishing the major part of his narrative. Once he has given this subjective account of their affair—throughout which he behaved both lovingly and cruelly toward Rebekka—he adds fragments of her diary from the earliest days of their relationship and then her crucial letter to him in which she explains her behavior, absolves him of guilt, and leaves him a cross woven out of strands of her hair. He uses Rebekka's diary and letter as an alternative, objective voice; but in fact she speaks in his. Finally he concludes his narrative with a description of the new found peace conferred upon him by his dead lover. Far from the formless manuscript he claims to be writing, *The Cross* is a carefully structured interpretation of his brief and stormy encounter with Rebekka, his subsequent loss, and his gain of a vision of eternal life.

Like the couples of "Liv" and "The Plain," the narrator and Rebekka, responding to something innocent, sad, and mysterious in each other, feel they have met their destiny. But there is another crucial force in their affair, and that is a third party, a sculptor named Bredo whom the narrator meets at approximately the same time as he meets Rebekka. The two men are as close as the two men of the early poem, "Friends," a perfect balance for each other. Bredo, the personification of the brooding 1890s artist, inspires the narrator with two of the 1890s' most important aesthetic principles: one, there is a female spirit in the world, the spirit of creativity, inspiration and art, and therefore all women are one woman; and two, one must pay a great price for creativity. Rebekka, of course, becomes the embodi-ment—and the victim—of this spirit, making through her love and her death a religious work of art of the narrator's life.

The narrator would like to bring his two friends together, almost as if he were anxious to bring harmoniously together the various aspects of himself, the child, the woman, the artist, the man. But Rebekka is most unwilling to meet Bredo. The narrator tells his story in such a way that we, the readers, realize what the unsuspecting narrator at the time did not, i.e., that Rebekka had been Bredo's model and inspiration. Rebekka's latent spirit in the sculptor is, of course, why the narrator is so drawn to him in the first place. But her former relationship will also become the major source of the narrator's intense jealousy.

With his two friends supposedly not having met, the narrator and Rebekka move into the country, where they spend four months, one idyllic and the others increasingly difficult. Rebekka begins to make trips into the city. The narrator follows her, unable to help himself, and discovers that she sees Bredo from time to time. He assumes that they are having an affair, but it is later disclosed that he has misjudged the situation. She in fact goes to town to visit her child, we assume by Bredo. At home the narrator and Rebekka never confront each other, but he begins to treat her as if his jealous interpretation of events were true. In his immense ego-centrism he finds it intolerable that she should have belonged to someone else. He is cold and unkind, he finds her disgusting, and he refuses to speak to her. But his mood can change in a moment, from this cruelty to love; and so he vacillates between the extremes of love and hate.

But although he might love her, he is a pawn of his own terrible jealousy, which grows more and more powerful until it reaches its climax in what appears to be a nightmare about an old man claiming to be Rebekka's first husband. He tortures the narrator with images of his raw sexual relationship to her.

—Tell me . . . have *you* kissed . . . have *you* kissed . . . ha, it's such a lovely little innocent one . . . have *you* kissed . . . it's on the left side . . . just under her breast . . . Have *you* kissed . . .

He stood right up close to me, he stared at me, he bent down to my ear, he blew a word into it, it still rings inside.(100–101)

The narrator and Rebekka grow more and more estranged, but near the end he repents and goes home to find her. The house, however, stands empty and Rebekka is dead. She has left him a letter in which she explains that he must not grieve for she was meant to die. She calls him her god. She says that she was born for his sake and that through him she experienced life's ultimate beauty. She leaves him a cross of her hair so that he will know "the purest, highest love" (115).

It has been essential for the narrator to show—to himself and to us—that he acted in the most noble, aesthetic, and religious spirit when he gave himself over to his feelings, be they passionate or indifferent, of love or of hate. Early in the relationship he decided to allow himself to be acted upon by fate in whatever form. "I became like an open church waiting to embrace the sound of the psalm. It might be a wedding psalm and it might be a requiem" (64). As the relationship progressed and he became ever more caught in his schizophrenic swings of emotion, he desperately adhered to the same principle. He believes religiously in the passivity of the autumnal man, choosing to yield to the life forces, interpreted here as the strong and contradictory feelings inspired in him by Rebekka; and indeed, through her love and her death his life is transformed.

He ends his narrative with a vision of the sun which has become not the dreaded light of the dawn but an image of life-giving blood, the feminine spirit on earth and in man. "In the morning when the sun rises red above the sea turning it into the blood that waters the earth,—then my breast is filled with the need to create, to strew seeds and sparks around me for every day of life" (118).

"The Unknown One"

"Den ubekjendte" [The Unknown One, III:180–88], a short prose sketch written in the late spring of 1895, provides a fitting closure for the discussion of the fiction.[20] It is a further illustration of the poet/narrator's aesthetic use of the woman as a medium through which to make his world more meaningful and his need then to free himself of her through a metaphorical death ritual.

The story takes place in Paris, the city the narrator has experienced as "this idiotic labyrinth of streets" (182) until one day, as he is sitting on a bench in Luxembourg Park, he notices a woman about whom "there was not the slightest trace of anything unusual" (180). But he follows her, convinced that he must hear her speak, that he must watch her eat cherries that very evening in a restaurant before the lamps are lit. He grows more and more excited by his fantasy of their beautiful evening. "It would be immoral of me if I ate alone this evening, immoral" (181). Yet he is unable to approach her, remaining rigidly passive as she disappears into the crowd. But even as she slips farther and farther away from him, the city, once full of chaos and idiocy, becomes a more beautiful and a more human place. The ordinary woman, whom the poet invests with the power of the extraordinary, transfigures the city.

One day he sees her again from his window and, unable to think of anything else, he rushes down the stairs.

Something cried in me: You must get hold of her, you must know everything about her, and you must confide in her, confide in her of yourself. She must share your shame. You and she must sit together all afternoon. You must sit in the dusk and hold her hand. And then you will see clearly into all of Paris, out into the whole world. (186)

He is gripped, however by the same passivity, the seconds pass, and she walks away.

But even though she disappears a second time, it seems that she has fundamentally altered his perspective. Luxembourg Park has become the poetic embodiment of the human temperament to which he is most attracted, mysterious, changeable, and beautiful. One morning he is drawn to the park, only to realize that it is crying. In that moment he loves the park as the narrators have always loved their sad women. "I lost myself in it. It became so infinitely large. It was a virgin forest that swallowed all of Paris" (187–88). He walks to the park bench where he originally saw the woman and finds her lying there asleep. As he looks at her he thinks of all the costly hours life meant them to have but are gone forever; and he muses that he had let her go off alone, unprotected, while he had given so much of his time to others. But he does not blame himself. He bends down and looks at her for a long time and then says, "I saw that it was the first time" (188). He fears he has awakened her, holds his breath, but sees that she sleeps and walks away.

The implication, of course, is that she became a prostitute during the night. Once made absolutely innocent by the poet through her ordinariness, she has now been defiled and thus is dead to him. Although no actual death occurs, the final image of her lying asleep on the park bench is unquestionably an image of death. Like all the narrators—of "Liv" and "The Plain" and *The Cross*, and the poetry, too—this narrator uses the woman as his inspiration only to transfer his feelings and longings for her into something beyond her, envisioning his solitary, metaphysical communion with nature in sexual terms. He is safe and secure in the large, virgin forest of his mind.

Chapter Six

The Plays

The Form

In 1896 Obstfelder wrote to a friend, "It's very possible, by the way, that I'm becoming, more and more, a dramatist; there is no form that comes so naturally to me."[1] It is curious that he should have been so enthused about the dramatic form in particular. For him the essence of life and literature lay in the invisible movements of the soul, in silences and obscurities. Drama, however, is not generally made of such sensitive stuff; but Obstfelder, if not under the influence of, then once again in the spirit of the Symbolists, attempted to make mood the real protagonist in the theater.

He completed three plays and the first act of a fourth. In the crucial year of 1892 when he started to think of himself as a poet again, he began his first legitimate play, *Esther,* and from then on he always seemed to have a dramatic work—more or less close at hand—that he was contemplating, beginning, reworking, or finishing. In this sense the plays span nearly the decade of his career. In terms of his enthusiasm for the drama, however, they figure most centrally in the years between late 1895 and 1900.

Obstfelder was never able to complete the one-act play *Esther* to his satisfaction. He started it in 1892, is known to have been working on it in 1893 and 1894, but did not publish it until 1899.[2] His second one-act play, *Om våren* [In Spring] is undated. Hannevik thought it likely that it was begun in the years 1895–1896. It was accepted by the National Theater in Oslo in 1899 and first performed in 1902.[3] Obstfelder's most significant play is *De røde dråber* [The Red Drops], written in part for the internationally known Norwegian actress Johanne Dybwad. Begun in the winter of 1895–1896, the first version of the play was finished by the following fall and submitted to the Christiania Theater but was sent back to Obstfelder for rewriting. He finished the second version of the play in the fall of 1897, and although unsuccessful in getting it performed in Christiania, he published it that same year.[4] Its first known performance was in 1928. In the late winter/early spring of 1900 Obstfelder began work on *Den sidste konge* [The Last King], of which he completed only the first draft of Act I and the beginning of Act II. Only Act I is published in the collected works.

Obstfelder's plays are as successful, or unsuccessful, as most of the plays written in the tradition of the so-called "static" drama. He shared with the major Symbolist dramatists, of whom Maurice Maeterlinck was the major representative, a desire to communicate in the theater as they did in their poetry, through suggestion, mood, and deliberate obscurity. Their plays flew in the face of any traditional concept of dramatic action, replacing character, plot, and development with the favored musical structure of mood, theme, and variation. All elements of the drama were to contribute to the mysterious mood.

The motivation for the static drama was, as Maeterlinck himself defined it, to portray "the soul, self-contained in the midst of everrestless immensities."[5] The intention was no less than to relocate the dramatic conflict, as the most universal drama was deemed present in the silent soul. Maeterlinck's often-quoted example is of the old man in the armchair.

> I have grown to believe that an old man, seated in his armchair, waiting patiently with his lamp beside him, giving unconscious ear to all the eternal laws that reign about his house, interpreting, without comprehending, the silence of doors and windows, and the quivering voice of the light, submitting with bent head to the presence of his soul and destiny— . . . I have grown to believe that he, motionless as he is, does yet live in reality a deeper, more human and more universal life than the lover who strangles his mistress, the captain who conquers in battle, or "the husband who avenges his honor."[6]

Although direct influence is difficult to demonstrate, Obstfelder was undoubtedly aware of Maeterlinck's theories. In a letter to Johanne Dybwad which accompanied the original manuscript of *The Red Drops* he formulated his dramatic method in terms not unlike Maeterlinck's. The details refer specifically to *The Red Drops,* but the general principles apply equally to his two earlier plays. He said he imagined a theater of poetry, a theater in which the audience would experience the play as it would a landscape painting or a piece of beautiful music; and he too spoke of the altered focus of the drama.

One might think then that the dramatic conflict is that which takes place between [the protagonist]and [the characters which surround him]. This is not the case. What happens dramatically to [him] happens only in terms of himself. And that is what should be new and crazy or new and good, and for a good actor, the interesting task.

These other people exist only as background, as "the chorus," in relation to which [the main characters] should stand out as large silhouettes, poeticized over some of life's great forces.[7]

In the plays—as consistently elsewhere—Obstfelder sought to present not ordinary characters on an ordinary stage, but the "essential" human being in an eternal perspective. To this effect atmosphere overwhelms, dialogue is minimal but pregnant with meaning, silence is everywhere and movement—save for fleeing the stage—is slight. The individual characters seem pathetically small and fragile, prisoners of the mood that envelops them. Time and space, life and death, as projected through the mood, seem omnipotent; and thus the powerlessness of the individual could be dramatically portrayed, were the play successful.

There are obvious risks in this kind of theater. Silences, in and of themselves, are not dramatic. Too little action can be simply tedious. Striving for the "inexpressible," Obstfelder often employed the utterly simple, yet pregnant vocabulary of the poetry; but the effect could be melodramatic or banal.

Nevertheless, the plays are an interesting segment of Obstfelder's authorship. In particular, they demonstrate his constant fascination with the theme of rebirth cast in ever-changing symbols. The same ritualistic pattern, fundamental to the prose, of descending into the darkness in order to be spiritually reborn is also central to these plays, particularly *The Red Drops*. They provide, in fact, a review of Obstfelder's works from the early poetry to *A Cleric's Journal*, containing as they do the major symbolic constructs of his poetic universe.

Esther

The play (I:189–210)[8] is an eerie enactment of a man's rescue from insanity by a cold goddess figure named Esther. Begun in 1892, it seems to be a poetic distillation of the sequence of emotional stages which led to Obstfelder's personal recovery from mental illness, that is to say, at any rate, the emotional stages reflected in his poetry in 1892 and 1893. The man—pale, freezing, sick, unnamed—follows Esther in out of the storm. Barely able to speak, he says, in effect, that he has lost his identity. ". . . I have nothing to tell . . . I *am* nothing . . . I am crossed out . . . I am mad. (Suddenly:) Don't you see: I am mad? . . ." (198). He sought meaning—continuity and correspondences— but he found none. Using an image familiar from the "America Journal," he says he had dreamed of being imbued with the essence of life. "I thought it would come as on great, wide wings, it would come and sing in me and lift my steps high above the ground" (200). He discovered, however, that it was all of his "own mind's making" (200), and he grew sick and mad from despair. He longs now for the peace of death, "something ice-cold." (200). It is precisely this coldness he sensed in Esther as he saw her walking along the shore in the storm, and he followed her, he says, simply because he "had to" (195). Esther, in her cold and noble peace, exists in a twilight land between life and death, "earth and stars" (206), and in this frigid kingdom the man takes refuge and is reborn.

Obstfelder personally sought refuge in a poetry of death-like calm following his recovery. "Barcarole," "I See," "Without Name," and "Eve" all take place in that amorphous land of ominous shadows, blues, and grays. Esther is, though, the most dramatic of the women from the blue abyss. Like them she is both nurturing and threatening: she speaks warmly, but of coldness; she wished to be a mother but is instead a frigid queen. Ultimately, however, she aids the poet as the others could not. Eve's eyes reveal only emptiness, the prostitute holds the poet's head against her breast, and Elvi rocks him to sleep; but Esther sends him back into the world.

The familiar paradox that the poet can be reborn only through the power of the death goddess is the crux of the play, consistently informing its mood, imagery, and characters.[9] The scene opens onto a

living room at midnight, i.e., neither yesterday nor today. The
furniture suggests "noble warmth" (191) but the room is bathed in
shadowy *green* light. A hail storm rages outside. Esther enters, coming
in from the storm. Her bearing and her costume suggest peace and
elegance, but with her first words she identifies herself with the
violence of the ice storm. "I like storms. . . . It is hail. (As she warms
her hands at the stove.) Oh how it tears and pulls at my veil . . . It is
like hands. *Strong* hands" (191–92). Again contrary to her peaceful
bearing, she calls emphatically and hysterically for wine, saying to her
companion, "Let us be happy, Lina! (Jumps up.) Mad! Let us drink
wine! . . . Wine, yes! Storms and wine, they go together! And large,
green glasses!" (192–93). Esther leaves the room and returns dressed
in a white dressing gown and black shawl, again accentuating her
paradoxical nature. Her next lines reveal a woman both contemptuous
and desirous of men, in her hatred and her intensity reminiscent of the
sadomasochistic women of the early poetry.

> . . . Have you ever . . . have you ever let man-hands loosen your hair . . .
> those coarse hands crumpling your tresses? . . . (In a changed voice.)
> Nonsense!
> There are no men. . . . There is a despondency over the earth that is
> sucking the marrow out of people. . . .
> I wanted the man who would pray to me! Who would throw himself on
> his knees in anguish. He is pursued. He has no place to lay his head. (In a
> rigid voice.) Nonsense. Never.
> Never shall those stupid, raw lips touch me! Never! (193)

As if in answer to her mad prayer, a man pursued and in anguish
comes out of the storm and does fall down at her feet. She understands
him, for she too has retreated from life out of profound disappoint-
ment. She gives no explanation, but her earlier monologue suggests it
had to do with men and love and loss of innocence. She has sought
refuge in what she calls her "death." "My great, blue, wonderful
peace!" (201). Now she is "the woman hidden in life's shadows"
(202), her children unborn. But though her loneliness is warmer to
her than the warmth of men, she fears for the man who is following
in her path of death. "You *must* not! You must live! Go out! See the
sun!" (203)

Now follows a mysterious birth scene in which Esther, the queen of death, gives life to the man. Throughout the scene Esther is referred to as "She," the man as "He," as if to suggest that their personalities momentarily merge until the end of the play when Esther is left alone on the stage, and is once again called by her name. Esther and the man also continually exchange places, first she kneeling for him, then he for her, indicating, perhaps, a transfer of power. Ironically, at the crucial moment when the poet quickens to life, Esther is sitting like a child on his lap. They fall then into a passionate kiss, Esther becoming at one and the same time mother, lover, and child.

She inspires life in the man by her own brief, ecstatic reawakening. As the women of the fiction undergo a death ritual, Esther undergoes a birth ritual to release the man from the grip of death. She takes him to the window and points to the world outside, a world of frost-covered trees and endless blue in which everything sleeps. But then she sees her blue world as it begins to thaw, describing it in imagery reminiscent of the reawakening of life in "All Creation Sighs." Esther grows ecstatic, remembering the burning sun. As if in a trance she hears the laughter of children, and becomes like a child herself, calling the poet to follow. They kiss, and when they part the poet witnesses the miracle of birth in Esther's eyes. He sees in them what he could not see in Eve's, the earth springing from a flower bud; and thus Esther, who never gave birth to children, gives birth to the world in miniature. The man takes his leave of her to reenter life, but Esther remains behind.

Fittingly, the play ends in a pantomime as Esther sinks back into her cold, blue peace. She takes out a pistol, fingers it and lays it aside; then she fetches a watering can and waters the flowers. Is she choosing the symbol of life over death? Or is she canceling out one with the other? The latter seems the most correct. She unbuttons the bodice of her dress and puts her hand inside, fingering her breast as she had the pistol, and she says, "Should have nursed children. . . . Ice cold. . ." (210). The play ends in this tableau of frigidity.

Esther and the man are not so much characters as states of mind or moods, two aspects of one personality, perhaps. There being no logical or psychological explanation for the changes they work on each other, it is most helpful—particularly in light of the plays that follow—to view their interaction "alchemically" as two imperfect substances that momentarily commingle to form gold, i.e., the whole personality. Seen as the descent of the soul into darkness in order to recover itself, the soul of this play, suffering from despair, enters Esther's kingdom of blue death, where it is made whole.

Yet once again, Obstfelder seems at odds with himself. The symbols of the play announce that rebirth has occurred. The sun is rising, Esther is like a child, and the flower blooms. The moment of transcendence, however, is false, forced into being by Obstfelder's insistence that it happen, like the ecstatic dance in "Tempest," and it is quickly forgotten as Esther repossesses the stage. Obstfelder undoubtedly intended her character to represent a stage toward transcendence. "Your eyes, in between earth and the stars" (206), the man says. But although he is able to move beyond her, Obstfelder is not. She is the eternal force in the play, powerfully drawn and in command of the stage from beginning to end. Her deadly passivity lingers long after the man has gone out to reenter life, blue chills the gold of the sun, and the laughter of children seems only an echo. At this time, Obstfelder could not escape from these women of the abyss.

In Spring

Spiritual rebirth is also the theme of Obstfelder's second one-act play, *In Spring* (I:211–49). This is as gentle, warm, and quiet a drama as *Esther* is cold and stormy. It is akin in mood to the prose poem "Housewife," in which a middle-aged woman is reawakened by a tear and a butterfly. The play is set in a garden on an evening late in spring. It is the time of the white nights when darkness never falls. The wind blows imperceptibly, the flowers are fragrant and lush, and in the background someone is softly playing a folk song on the piano. Herr Winge and the Widow Ring meet "accidentally" in this flower garden after twelve years. Their reunion is a triumph of sorts for Winge, a poet who had loved Fru Ring from afar but never dared tell her, only silently confessing his love in a poem. "But one day,/ when I have bathed in the Ganges' river,/ then I will,/ see her, awaken her, speak to her" (241). She barely noticed Winge then, married Ring, lived a good life for twelve years, and has recently been widowed. During this spring reunion she and Winge fall in love, but in a far more profound way than they could have when they were younger. Essentially guided by Winge, the two experience at least the initial stages of the awakening prophesied in his poem. Truly a mystical poet's fantasy fulfilled, the poem itself now acts as the catalyst or elixir for spiritual rebirth.

In Spring may be Obstfelder's true hymn to life. It is, at any rate, one of the most positive pieces he ever wrote. The relationship between the man and the woman is mutual, caring, and virtually free of conflict. Unlike any of the other protagonists involved in a love affair, Winge is a completely life-affirming character, having apparently emerged well and whole from a period of great pain, undoubtedly insanity and the blue death. He demands no sacrificial death from the woman and is connected with no death imagery, save the utter passivity of the end. He believes in life and, more importantly, in life's ability to renew itself continually.

It is Fru Ring who feels that something has died in her. She appeals to Winge to confirm her fears, but he insists the seed of life cannot die. Groping for words to interpret her unrest, Winge tells her she has need of something that makes daily life "religion, something with angels in it" (219). Using the simplest of language, he describes essentially a monistic vision of reality.

... something which is only *one*,—where there are not two things,—as if one in front and one in back, one that you see and one that you never understand. Something that is neither too high nor too low, but right here, around you, around you, in you, always. (219)

The "drama" of the play lies in the gentle interaction between Winge and Fru Ring, he inspiring her, then she him, as they begin to feel one with the rhythms of spring, with each other, and with themselves. When the moment is close at hand each projects a different image of the experience of oneness. For Winge it is something solid and white. "Something luxuriant has come—a great, flowing white drapery" (243). For Fru Ring it is liquid and transparent, a boiling stream within her, the holy water of the Ganges River flowing over her head, ears, and throat. In the end the two sit as one, waiting for "Happiness" to possess them. Fru Ring says, "almost inaudibly,"

He is coming.
. . . Happiness. Something that breathes over the earth, emits a fragrance under the skin and makes your cheeks tremble. (248)

About to be reborn, Winge and Fru Ring await Happiness—or perhaps God—like a fearful, expectant virgin awaiting her lover.

There also exists a subtler set of symbols that conveys the process of rebirth of Winge and Fru Ring. In the play following this one, *The Red Drops,* the protagonist is an alchemist. Already in *Spring,* however, Obstfelder seems to have consciously, if not obviously, employed alchemical images. Fru Ring is the central figure. Her name means ring or circle, and as Jung has explained, the alchemical vessel was always round "so that what comes out of the vessel shall be equally 'round,' i.e., simple and perfect like the *anima mundi.*"[10] Her name symbolizes the state of oneness to which she and Winge are about to return. Interestingly, his name, which means "wings," calls up Obstfelder's personal image of God coming in the form of great white wings which he used in the "America Journal" and other writings inspired by his illness. If Winge is connected to spirit, Fru Ring is connected to matter. She is linked to two flowers, the white apple blossoms of spring and a metaphorical murky-red bloom. White and red are central, alchemical colors, associated with the so-called Mercury of Philosophers or First Matter, thought to be the basic substance to which all metal had to be reduced before it could be transmuted. Ring is associated with the yellow dandelion, yellow being the color of sulphur, the substance that mixed properly with mercury would produce gold. The transformation of Winge and Ring thus implies the union of spirit and matter, god and man, the solid and the liquid, sulphur and mercury becoming gold.

In *Esther* rebirth occurred, albeit forcedly. In *Spring* it is only about to occur, but the expectation of Winge and Fru Ring is true. In *The Red Drops* rebirth has become a mystery once again, the secret the adept tries to learn. The play is also Obstfelder's best.

The Red Drops

The Red Drops (I:99–183) was the play that inspired Obstfelder to say that the dramatic form came more naturally to him than did any other. He simply could not conceal his excitement for this work. In the hope of interesting Johanne Dybwad in the part of Lili, he sent her the manuscript in the fall of 1896, and in his accompanying letter included a lengthy commentary. Obstfelder seldom presumed to discuss his own works critically, but he was deeply concerned that this one be understood. ". . . I know—even if it can never be performed—that it is not just an ordinary work. Don't misunderstand these words! There is more sadness than self-praise and conceit in them."[11]

Compared to *Esther* and *Spring*, *The Red Drops* is the longest—four acts—and the most performable. It also has a larger cast: Odd Berg, his father, his fiancée, Borghild, his assistant, Lili, and a host of minor characters; but like the earlier plays, *The Red Drops* is essentially about the conflict of one, not many. As Obstfelder wrote to Ms. Dybwad: "What happens dramatically to Odd happens only in terms of himself. And that is what should be new and crazy or new and good, and for a good actor, the interesting task."[12]

Rebirth is once again at the heart of the drama, but as if going backwards in time, it is a miracle to be rediscovered, not a miracle experienced, as in *Esther*, or imminently awaited, as in *Spring*. The play belongs to Odd Berg, the alchemist destined to search for the beginning of life, symbolized in his red, liquid brew. He is portrayed as an immensely lonely and suffering man doomed to choose to investigate a dark and forbidden world, although the people would prefer to have him among them as their heroic leader, and he, in a very real sense, would prefer to *remain* among them. Obstfelder wrote about him:

It is not at all my intention to portray *Odd* as a *martyr* for these common people. To the contrary, he really disappoints them. . . . But he is pursued by the ideal, by immense feelings of human pain and imperfection, and his great duty to beauty. He is *pursued*, and he suffers—he *suffers* by disappointing the people of his town, but he *must*. . . . He is condemned—condemned precisely by this terrible inclination imbedded in him, the inclination toward the superhuman, the divine.[13]

The fatalism of *The Cross*, written within the same time period, is present in *The Red Drops*. In the novella the protagonist puts himself on trial in order to prove that he could not, indeed should not, have acted otherwise. In the play Odd is psychologically torn between a commitment to life and devotion to his dream, but actually he has no choice, for it is in his blood to be the bearer of the dream. His father, long an alchemist in secret, says to him toward the end of the play: "A dream is passed from generation to generation. And he who feels *the dream* within, among human beings feels the mark of Cain on his forehead. But when *death* nears, then he sees that— —the truth, it was—the dream" (177–78).

Odd Berg is initially drawn as a schizophrenic stereotype, a feted engineer of the new century, a scorned alchemist of the old; but the labels are intended to be obvious so as not to detract from the essence of Odd, i.e., the profound pain inherent in his helpless vacillation between life and the dream. He is seriously tempted by them both. Fittingly they appear as two women, Borghild, Odd's fiancée, who belongs to earth, and Lili, his alchemical assistant, who belongs to the spirit. The dynamic of the play lies in Odd's oscillation between the worlds of Borghild and Lili. In Act I he flees from Borghild and the people who are about to honor him as the engineer of the future. In Acts II and III he is with Lili in his dark laboratory. Lili dies at the end of Act III, and in Act IV he has inexplicably returned to Borghild. In the final scene, however, he is lured from her arms by the apparition of Lili.

Borghild is queen of the earthly symbols of perfection and fulfillment. She is associated with the color red, with roses, with the sun, and full breasts. She *is* the substance of the red elixir. She demands Odd's commitment and condemns him when he cannot give it.

Lili is a child of that blue world of death that is more than life. She is very much like Liv, fragile, virginal, and dying. As Borghild is watched over by the sun, she is watched over by the stars. Obstfelder wrote of her:

Lili, strange, with her trembling sense of beauty,—everything *Odd* says she must change into beautiful pictures in order to understand,—I have not *at all* thought of her as *ugly* for ex.—near death, but an expression for everything tremblingly, quiveringly human.[14]

Lili demands nothing, grateful for acceptance, ecstatic over Odd's chaste kiss as she is dying; yet she commands his soul.

Lili and Odd are spiritual siblings, and he therefore feels most at peace with her. She is his link to the world beyond death. It is to Lili he confides his dream of finding the first law of life, of rearranging what he calls the atoms of life so that the human spirit can be "rebuilt" in harmony with itself. Lili not only listens to Odd's dream, she begins to undergo it physically. As she is dying, she is in a state of decomposition or transition between the living and the dead. Her vision seems to indicate that some sort of transformation or "rearrangement" is taking place.

When I close my eyes and hold my hands in front of them I see so many wonderful things, all kinds of marvelous colors, and pentagons, and hexagons, and stars, and diamonds, and always new ones, and they go up and down. Do you think it is like this when you die? (137–38)

Although fiercely attracted to Borghild, Odd is always anxious around her, inexplicably frightened by her red world. In Act I a group of women wish to present him—the man of action—with a bouquet of red roses, but he hesitates, forcing Borghild to accept them for him. In the last act the color red seems almost to suffocate him. Once again he is to be honored by his people: he has renounced his alchemical dream as witchery and is about to give himself to Borghild's world of roses and sun. For the occasion Borghild and the minor characters are dressed in red, but the density of the color so frightens Odd that he must leave the room. He is alien in her world, so much so that although he is heralded as the hero of the new age, he never speaks of its coming. That is left to the minor characters whom Odd mocks through his silence and his secret occupation.

Odd's tragedy is that he cannot give himself fully to either Borghild or Lili, nor is he able to bring about a synthesis of those two aspects of himself. Lili knows that if he is to find the elixir of life—his harmony of soul—he must bring together Borghild's world and her own. He must add something blue to the red liquid; "It isn't enough to gather up the sun, you must gather up the stars, too!" (149). That a synthesis of Borghild and Lili is the secret solution seems to be indicated by

their association with earth and spirit, woman and child, and also with
the alchemical colors red (Borghild, of course) and white (Lili, by
virtue of her purity and her name); but Odd seems barely aware of his
task, vacillating between the one and the other with not even a
symbolic effort to bring them together in harmony. With unconcealed
exasperation, Arne Hannevik has written of this play:

> The only thing left is the strong inner tension in the protagonist's labile
> mind between two attitudes which do not allow themselves to be reconciled
> or subordinated to a higher principle. . . . Therefore one must assume that
> Odd Berg will continue in the same vascillation even after the play is finished.
> If in fact his last experience was not so strong that his mind gave way
> completely.[15]

Odd's last experience is indeed obscure. As he is speaking to the
crowd which has come to honor him he grows silent and pale, and
flees. In a scene reminiscent of the early erotic poetry, Borghild
attempts to hold him in her earthly spell. She commands him to his
knees and asks, "Who *am* I, Odd?" "Am I your goddess?" "Am I the
only one on earth?" (180–81). Odd is barely able to recognize her, as
if a stronger spell had been cast upon him. The play ends as the
terrified Odd sees an apparition of Lili, white and radiant, standing
where Borghild had just stood. The ending is unclear. Is Odd about to
die? His father had said that in the presence of death the dream is seen
as the truth. Or has a synthesis of some sort occurred between Lili and
Borghild in that for a split second they might have occupied the same
place? This does not seem likely.

As Hannevik said, Odd will probably vacillate impotently between
the one extreme and the other. The theme is a familiar one in
Obstfelder's work, central particularly to the poetry in verse, even to
the point of being the organizing principle of *Poems*. During the
middle years it seems to have occupied Obstfelder less as he wrote
pieces in one dominant mood, like "Liv," "The Plain," and *Spring*. In
The Cross and *The Red Drops* it reemerges as important, and it is to
be the most central principle—thematic and structural—of *A Cleric's
Journal*. The soul swinging helplessly between two extremes is, of
course, the perfect image for Obstfelder's existential sense of homeless-

ness. The nightmarish unrest this vacillation causes is perhaps the most dominant mood of *The Red Drops*. But Obstfelder also seemed to feel that only by submitting to the spell of the extremes could the soul hope to achieve a new harmony.

The Last King

In the spring of 1900 Obstfelder was working on the draft of a play entitled *Den sidste konge* [The Last King, I:251–99]. He completed Act I and had begun Act II (not published in the collected works). The play is too incomplete to warrant an analysis, but it can be used to demonstrate Obstfelder's increasing concern for the legitimacy of the poet in society.[16] According to the first act, the play is about a young king torn between a fanatic desire humbly and completely to serve his people and a profound need to find peace and isolation in some protective place. As in *The Red Drops* Obstfelder, if not questions, then writes an apology for the poet's role in society, for as Odd was a poet disguised as a scientist/alchemist, this man is a poet disguised as a king. The anonymous protagonist is, in the later works, given an honored occupation or title, scientist, king, and, in *A Cleric's Journal*, minister. All are in some sense the gods of earth, the leaders of their age. But though they wish to serve in the world they are helpless to do so. They are too fragile, too misanthropic, and too in love with beauty and death; yet they are in principle so committed to life that they cannot allow themselves to be poets without guilt. They are emotionally homeless men, unable to come to rest in either extreme of their personality. As the king says to an old woman, his mother figure in the play:

Where is a king at home? I am *not* at home in there. And when I . . . see the lines of your face, then it is as if there is something deep inside me that I don't dare listen to because it is dead, dead forever, or more correctly, because it *must* be dead, *shall* be dead. (295)

Chapter Seven

The Diary Novel

A Cleric's Journal

Although Obstfelder had had such enthusiasm for *The Red Drops*, he eventually came to believe that *En prests dagbog* [A Cleric's Journal, II:121–234][1] would be his greatest work; but in spite of the fact that he labored over it for three years, he was not able to complete it. His difficulty with the *Journal* is not surprising given the treacherous nature of his major source material, i.e., his mental breakdown, and the moral seriousness with which he approached his art in general. The task simply became monumental. Already in 1893 when he first conceived of the idea of writing a novel based on his illness, he wrote to his brother that the Norwegian author Arne Garborg (1851–1924) called it his "duty" to write the work;[2] and the more and the longer he wrote, the more painful his sense of responsibility toward the *Journal* became, depriving him of any real peace of mind. In a letter to a friend, probably from 1897, he said:

But I don't get much rest and peace, I am driven, driven, and I get no rest from this sad book that fate has apparently decided I must write. I never thought it was so painful to be a writer,—so great an offer—so great a feeling of responsibility.[3]

The *Journal* was long on Obstfelder's mind. He wrote his brother for the Frogner letter in the summer of 1893, remarking parenthetically, "You understand I need those things I can get from the time of the fresh wounds,"[4] but he did not actually begin the book until 1895, at approximately the same time as *The Red Drops*. For a while the play had demanded the greater part of his interest and certainly gave him greater satisfaction, but in 1897 he turned to the *Journal* and was preoccupied with it until his death in the summer of 1900. He often felt unequal to the task of writing it and as late as the spring of 1900 had grave misgivings. He wrote to Ellen Key in May, "... more and more a deep despondency has taken hold of me. I doubt what I have done. I don't think it corresponds to what I *wanted* to do, and what I still believe I *could* do."[5]

Obstfelder died with the manuscript unfinished, having written the first section and begun drafts of a second; but immediately following his death the first section was published as *A Cleric's Journal.*[6] Obstfelder himself obviously felt it was not ready for publication; and some critics—Hannevik included—consider it flawed, in particular by its lack of concentration and resolution. Indeed, the *Journal* is an imperfect work; but by virtue of its serious intent, its aesthetic and psychological concerns, and its moments of real poetry, it *is* Obstfelder's major work. The *Journal* is a culmination in yet another new form—the diary novel—of the dominant themes of his authorship: the effort to see beyond the veil of reality; the relentless questioning of existence; the sensation of alienation, or homelessness, within the self and without; the vacillation between one emotional extreme and the other; and the search for peace and death. The *Journal*'s lack of resolution, considered by some an aesthetic flaw, is in reality an aesthetic device:[7] it is the essence of this novel more than any other of Obstfelder's works, making it his most fascinating, and at the same time, most frightening statement on the relativity of perception.

The line between biography and fiction was never thinner than in the *Journal.* Many of the cleric's visions can be traced to the "events," hallucinatory and real, of Obstfelder's illness which he recorded at the time in the "America Journal" and in letters and jottings from Frogner Colony.

The partial record of the events leading up to his breakdown, the "America Journal," seems to have provided Obstfelder with some of the most significant source material, both in regard to content and form. Specific images, such as the presence of God as the beating of great wings, appear in both journals. But there are also more general parallels. Obstfelder and the cleric fight the same battles, reaching desperately outward to discover the secret of the universe and inward to learn the secret of the self. Both risk insanity for vision. Music, which is Obstfelder's obsession in the "America Journal," is one of the cleric's principal metaphors. And, too, their manic/depressive

personalities determine the nature of their quests and the vacillating
format of both their journals.

That the protagonist is a cleric or a minister is also undoubtedly
inspired by Obstfelder's illness which, at least in one of its manifesta-
tions, assumed the form of a religious crisis. He supposedly emerged
from the breakdown with a belief in a personal God.[8] Obstfelder
actually seemed in danger of being overwhelmed by the religious
dimension of the *Journal,* however. He intended it to be both a
psychological study of a modern soul and a religious/philosophical
work of depth. As he wrote to Ellen Key in 1900, "Yes, I had the
wildest dreams about probing deep into both the problem of God and
the drama of life—. . . ."[9] But the "problem of God" often overcame
both Obstfelder and his minister. In a letter from 1898 he described
the concerns of the *Journal:*

I have for many years . . . wished to find an expression for religious
brooding and battle . . . for the painful fumbling toward God and the
Innermost, for the magnificent sensation of God at certain moments, for the
battle between God and man, for the appalling feeling of being distanced
from the source, etc., etc.[10]

These certainly are the obsessions of the brooding cleric. It is both his
method and his madness to pose questions about the nature of God
and Satan, goodness and evil, life and death, first from one philosophical vantage point, then another, and then still another, until hopefully
he would reach clarity, what he calls "the little center" or the
"innermost."

First of all, his *method* of questioning is dangerous, if not deadly;
but this will concern all dimensions of the *Journal,* not simply the
religious. Secondly, his religious philosophy is naive, as if deliberately
oversimplified to be understood by a tortured mind. *Possibly* this was
intentional on Obstfelder's part. The cleric's philosophical pretentions
are mocked at the end by the mother goddess who appears to him in
the setting sun, proclaiming that all his abstract thought is as nothing
compared to her substance, color, and form. Fittingly, it is a triumph
of the visual and the sensual over the intellectual, in other words, a

vindication of Obstfelder's own poetry. Nevertheless, up until the end, both Obstfelder and his cleric are repeatedly overcome by the religious questions, and the *Journal*, as a work of literature, suffers. As if to deemphasize its religious aspect, Herman Obstfelder said in 1925 that his brother "regarded the work as an attempt to portray how a modern human being thinks and feels."[11] And indeed, the *Journal* is at heart, and at best, Obstfelder's final portrait of the sensitive, soul-searching, religiously inclined poet caught in the nightmare of his own mind.

As the beginning of the *Journal* the cleric embarks on Obstfelder's typical existential quest for vision. His first words are: "What will remain at the end of this book? Will I have come to any result? Will I have experienced clarity?" (123). Like the protagonist of *The Cross* and Odd in *The Red Drops*, the cleric's method is to entrust himself to the power of his labile emotional life, as if it alone were meant to determine the fate of his quest. His relinquishing of control must, on the one hand, be interpreted as a most courageous act which possibly will gain for him the actual *experience* of the mystery of life. For example, his ecstatic vision of eternal space is something he can feel happening inside his own body: "All around there is light, light bursting into colors, colors fluttering and flaming, living and dying, bursting into new colors, dancing in time with bodies and worlds like the veils in the dancers' hands" (186). He seeks the moment of fusion of his spirit with another—perhaps the moment remembered in the poem, "Friends"—and is willing to risk his sanity for it.

On the other hand, his giving up of control can be interpreted as a dangerously passive act. At times he seems little more than a medium, powerless to defend himself from the forces he senses from without: "All that swishing up there over the roof races through my brain, the thoughts of the multitudes, sighs, complaints, go through my heart, I writhe in my bed, I want to hide myself from it, I cannot" (160). The most extreme example of the cleric's pathological passivity is the hallucination—quoted earlier in connection with the prose poems—during which he feels his body being invaded by ugly thoughts.

The cleric is obviously at great risk whether he should achieve transcendence and gain total self or suffer reduction to a completely passive state and lose his self. In either case the self is in danger, and the cleric therefore lives in dread of what he most desires, of "seeing

God." Several times he feels the nearness of God but at the crucial moment he is afraid to open his eyes, afraid to "see."

He envisions "a part of" God within himself as a foreign inner eye. Twice in earlier days, he says, he saw God inside him as a pupil, "older than myself, older than my mother, looking at me, looking" (156). We are reminded of Obstfelder's poem "Can the Mirror Speak?": ". . . looking at you with its deep, wise eye,/ —your own!" (I:31).

He lives in terrible fear that this other self, when he comes face to face with him, will say "you," in other words, will be *another*. But then again, he also fears that this other self will *not* be another. He is at times, too, comforted by the thought of the omnipresence of God and at other times tortured by it.

> I *want* to be alone here in my chamber. I cannot *stand* the thought that someone is looking at me uninvited.
>
> I was afraid of not meeting a soul of my soul. I tremble now at not standing there innermost face to face with one who is outside me, who will take my hand and call me "you." (158)

The minister's journey into himself is a terrible one, for there are no constants, no footholds, for the wandering, questioning self. One moment he is tempted to believe in the divinity of his own soul, the next so tortured by guilt he feels lowlier than a worm. God inspires in him joy but also terror, love but also hate. Even God is not a constant, the cleric interpreting him first as an objective, then a relative being. When he does "see" "Jahve" in a nightmare vision toward the end of the *Journal,* he discounts it as his "own nervousness," and, in essence, makes of himself a god by asking if the greater wonder of all is not the ability of the self "to create storms and movements and pains and dramas that are more than all earthly, daily life put together . . . ?" (228). The cleric's psyche and all it controls is as sifting sand. Nothing—be it an internal or external reality—has a constant value.

For example, the room in the city in which he lives and writes, his "chamber," is experienced interchangeably as a place of peace and disturbing unrest. It is a room with one window, sparely furnished, and with few comforts save for some books and a camelia. He jealously guards the room and its objects much like the young child/poet of "Christmas Eve," who carefully ordered his candle, Bible, and chest to protect himself from the chaos of the dark. The safe, ordered space of the chamber can, however, change instantaneously into chaos as the cleric imagines that God is everywhere, under his table and even on his paper, or that every inch of space in the room is in motion. He is denied—or denies himself—even a physical place of constancy and rest, his outer reality subject to his inner and no more stable than it is.

As was Odd, so too the cleric is homeless within himself. Typically he sees himself as the abandoned child in a chaotic universe. It is his most urgent wish to come to rest as a child under a stable sky. "I long for my childhood world. The sun that was over me then, the evening star that rose up over the greenwood, the grass I lay in" (178). Yet he is the *lost* child, walking "over the earth, over its curvature, my soul walks through all lands, and seas, and asks: Is there any soul that is like this one?" (134). He is the *abandoned* child. "It was as if I had been forgotten, alone on the earth, and everybody else were gone, and all the other planets were rolled away" (169).

The *Journal* itself is loosely divided into three sections. In the first the cleric vacillates between joy and depression, contemplating life's and his own divine and evil nature; in the second he sustains an ever-more ecstatic experience of the visions and rhythms of life; and in the third he once again vacillates between joy and depression until he encounters first the terrifying father god and finally the protective mother goddess. Most of the *Journal* "takes place" in his room and much of it in darkness; but every so often he sees "a current of sun rays" falling across the room through the window. If he could only follow it to its source, he thinks, for in the sun he believes he will find his lost home. It is the life from which he has been separated and becomes his journal's golden thread.

> I want to strain all my abilities to understand. There are after all times when I think a current of sun rays falls at an angle across my cell of darkness. I cannot follow it into its sun. My senses are not strong or rich enough, my body forbids it. But I can dimly perceive. And at any rate, I see at those moments better than I can otherwise with the five senses I have. (131)

Although he says he cannot, he does try to follow the light into its sun, encouraged by the memory of a transcendent experience in his past. Perhaps it *is* the moment remembered in the poem, "Friends," when the spiritual and corporeal fusion of two friends takes place in the spiraling fire of life, "an unending,—ringing—, firespiral,—/ which we cannot see the beginning of, and not the end of . . ." (I:4). Twice the cleric seems to penetrate into the source of the sun, the first vision occurring in the middle section of the *Journal*, the second at the very end of the third section. In the first he sees the "workings" of the universe as a spectacular dance of light waves and energy cells. In the second a woman appears to him in the midst of a rose sun. In both visions he finds, very briefly, a moment of rest, but he will find no home, for his mind knows none.

The essence of the cleric's first spectacular vision is eternal energy. Life in the universe, from the lowest to the highest form, lives as lines, arcs, and waves racing outward and back, crossing over each other, changing patterns. Cells give birth to cells that dance until they die. *Everything* is dancing, atom systems and sun systems; light bursts into colors, colors into flames, living and dying, moving in the rhythm of the universe.

The source of life is revealed to the cleric as constant motion. But if constant motion is life, it can also be, for the cleric, chaos. It is the curse of the modern world which he feels is being whipped as it races through space. "We see everything changing around us," he says. "We see nothing but change" (181). As his vision of the dancing universe threatens to turn in upon him he sees the earth as a nightmare of motion. Electric trains fly like lightning with millions of hearts in them, steam and gas drive the earth, money streams in an eternal flood through banks and stores, and monstrous hammers flame in the smoke of the earth.

Less important, however, than the content of these visions is the conflict they reveal. The cleric interprets motion alternately as life and death. Constant motion—energy or the life of the sun—can transform him, but he fears it can also destroy him. He imagines, for example, that everything in his body—the muscles and the blood—is moving and changing, so that it is never at rest. It is a terrifying thought to him, for it means chaos and death.

In contrast, he longs for and creates in musings and nostalgic dreams a safer, more peaceful world. He would like to go back to the stable universe of his childhood. He finds refuge—from time to time—in the order of his sparely furnished room. He paints a picture of a once constant world when time was steady, evenly measured by day and night, summer and winter. There were four elements, four seasons, four corners of the earth. Its shape was the square, not the circle, "the cornerless, endless form" (182). The sun rose in the ocean of the earth in the morning and came to rest there in the evening. The earth itself lay peacefully resting in its ocean on the columns of the four corners.

The cleric's longing for peace derives in part from his fear that the modern world is being driven mad by motion and the fear that he personally will be destroyed by it. Is our punishment our restless spirit? he asks. But he also comes dangerously close to wishing for death, wondering at one point if eternal peace might be filling our eyes with the same color, breathing, as he says, the same ether. Thus peace, like motion, can mean both life—particularly in the sense of freedom from chaos—and death. He sets for himself a very wicked trap indeed.

Seen in this light, the *Journal* is Obstfelder's final working out of his desire to live and his wish to sleep and die. Though the cleric may desperately wish to do so, he does not surrender his life. Rather he seeks to bring peace to motion, and this he does achieve in both his major visions, in the synthesis effectually finding a moment in time when he is at one with himself.

The cleric discovers that the key to the mystery of "motion at rest" is rhythm. His sudden awareness of such a rhythm in the universe saves his light vision from turning into chaos. He has grown frightened by the thought of the cells of his body in constant, invisible motion and the sight of the earth teaming with electricity, steam, gas, and monstrous hammers. "Finally you can be so tired of looking at it, of feeling it. It is as if all the hammers hammered at your own soft brain mass. . . . Is there then no longer any peace?" (191). He cannot control the confusion racing through his head. But then he hears a sound he does not know how to describe: perhaps an echo from a distant universe, or a mighty organ note, a sigh, a breath, a divine heart beat. Coming toward him from the stars, it pulses through him and through all that is. "One has of course spoken so many times about the rhythm of the universe, about the rhythm in the world. What good are words,—for that which passed through me was newer than all words!" (192). Rhythm orders the movement of the spirals, lines, arcs, atoms, and cells into a dance of life; and in the fusion of motion and rhythm the cleric discovers peace. It exists in a delicate balance, but it is, he understands, to be differentiated from stagnation, the true peace of death.

Significantly it is music, or more generally, rhythm, Obstfelder's secret language, that brings peace and vision to the cleric. Music as a motif is introduced earlier in the *Journal*, initially as a "sighing" from primitive forests which the cleric hears from time to time. It develops from descriptive metaphor to symbol early in the middle section of part two as the cleric, in need of rest, remembers that the Parcifal Overture had once seemed to him like the song of the universe, "a mighty chorus of great horns and strong strings, and still it didn't hurt my ears because it was a swelling harmony. There were no dissonances, nothing changed, it was eternally one and the same, and still it was not dead" (178–79).

The revelation of the music of the universe dominates the latter part of the cleric's vision; but it too is subject to his vacillating mind and therefore cannot remain constant. Through rhythm he is momentarily reconciled to life as motion. "A little earthly orchestra" becomes a microcosm for life and for art.

Art in stone was the art of the old world. Ours is art on leaping bows, on vibrating strings, on dancing air waves. We do not seek the beautiful repose, the fastened line. We seek the line before it is fastened, that which gave birth to the word and the form, change which is more eternal than matter. (194)

At first the orchestra is only a microcosmic analogy for life; but then the cleric sees the curtain drawn back to reveal the tabernacle of the world, and the universe *becomes* the orchestra. His sense of order, however, begins to slip away as he feels himself sitting in the midst of the orchestra unable to make out the individual instruments. Once again he has lost perspective. He longs for a sign from the composer, but wonders if he really exists.

Although the cleric deems rhythm to be the mysterious essence of peace in life, he is too frightened to look up when he feels it embrace him. At the peak moment when the "world rhythm" rushes through his body he feels, he says, as if "I should be forced to kneel, and still I didn't dare bend my knees!" (199). It is an ambivalent moment of exultation and humiliation, acceptance and rejection, wholeness and nothingness; but it is the beginning, he says, of life and truth.[12]

The cleric's mystical vision ends suddenly, giving birth to its opposite; and the darkness in which he now finds himself is as terrible as the light was magnificent. He awakens in the middle of the night. The light of the moon lies in a stripe across his room, illuminating it in such a way that it seems to him he has not seen it so clearly for a long time. Was the sun a fog? he asks. He feels a presence in the room as he had felt the presence of life, but it now comes from the underworld. A rat runs across the stripe of moonlight, ugliness and sin in animal form. It could block his vision, he says. "If I held it a few centimeters in front of my eyes, its dark sneaking body would block all suns and all universes" (204). The question of perspective reasserts itself in a grotesque way, the cleric recognizing both his subjective control over the darkness and its control over him. "Is there then a world that is completely hostile to the being of man?" he asks (204). It is the same question asked in the prose poem "The Arrow." "Are the powers of heaven challenged from the shadow realms?" (II:251). The rat seems to be an awful messenger, calling up another memory from this hellish region, a bedbug which, stinking of sin, invaded not only the cleric's room but his body.

In keeping with the ritualistic pattern of both the prose and the plays, the cleric, too, goes through his own hell to be reborn in the mother sun. Following the sight of the rat, he sees the world only in its ugliness. He calls it a huge toilet, where human beings and animals pour out their impurities. How do human beings exist in the filth? he asks. Cynically he sees them dressing themselves in silk, perfuming their hair, and powdering their faces in an effort to separate themselves from ugliness.

He then meets someone—a former schoolmate and a man who loves life—who chastens him. Bring your heaven down to earth, he says. Concentration on the transcendental, the invisible, and the otherworldly binds hands and hinders action. The greatest sin, he claims, is wasting the potential of the earth. The cleric is taken by him, not so much by his words—as he has often had the same thoughts—but by his face, for he believed so in his gospel of the earth. The cleric is momentarily inspired not to action, but to fantasy, imagining a new order of priests who would infiltrate all the institutions of the world, bringing the gospel of life to all. But though he is buoyed up by his fantasy for a while, he is not really a believer in a victorious humanity, free of sin and angst. A sadder vision tugs at his soul. "What was it all, that new, magnificent world one could dream about, what was it all compared to the mysterious, searching glance from misery's darkness?" (219). He is rooted in melancholy and finds it more profound.

Now his longing grows to see God, to come face to face with the other that will be like him or unlike him. His heart beats so alone. He therefore goes up into the mountains and there has two remarkable encounters, the one with a clearly masculine, deadly force, the other with the mother goddess of the sun. The theme of the child, desirous to be reunited with its parent, fittingly brings the *Journal,* and Obstfelder's work, to a close.

The first encounter is told in the past tense. I have been up there, the cleric says, but how will I tell about it. I have been sick, I have not dared think for many days, I have been frightened for my sanity. The experience he had is similar to the man's encounter with the satanic dog in the prose poem "The Dog," although the threatening force does not assume an animal form but comes as a storm, and out of the storm a thundering sound calling a name. "Was it Him?" the cleric asks. ". . . I know one thing, that I heard the ancient name roar across the whole plateau, around my ears and my soul and my heart, so that I believed it was death. Jahve" (224).

He had walked for a day and a night in a rugged, granite landscape of glaciers, black waters, and ice-cold rocks. The wind seemed alive and hostile, shouting threats in an age-old tongue into his mouth and nose. The penetration of his body begins. Something in the wind wanted him dead. He felt that whirling snow had been sent to throw him to the ground, but he fought back, rushing against the snow in jubilation.

He was aware of a large, dark cloud that might contain a spirit like his but greater than his. He was first frightened of it, but then challenged it, laughing in wild contempt. How could God expect him to understand if he did not know the language in which he spoke? The cloud seemed to answer with a violent rainstorm of thunder and lightning. As he dared not look up into the rhythm and light, he dared not now look up at the lightning, which came nearer as the name Jahve rolled in the thunder. The thunder rushed through his whole body, roaring "Jahve, Jahve." He lay face down on the ground, and closed his eyes, trying to close all the other eyes of his body, apparently a reference to all possible openings through which he might be entered. He felt something over him and dared not look. He feared it was death. Fire rushed through his body and he felt a searing pain in his hands and feet, as if a burning foot were treading on each of them. The incident is parallel to the man's hand being marked and bloodied by the dog. The burning wounds in the hands and feet may also suggest a parallel to Christ's stigmata. The cleric recounts that he must have lost consciousness, but he knew his whole body had struggled against death.

This masculine god is the enemy of life. He robs the cleric of consciousness and reduces him to a completely passive state, usurping control of his body and his soul. In the burning hands and feet there is the suggestion that the cleric, the son, is murdered by Jahve, or God the Father.

In retelling this nightmare, however, the cleric discounts it as a product of his own nervousness. He marvels, in fact, that he—his I— has managed to create such a terrible and magnificent storm. The nightmare is testimony to the mystery of the "I," out of which such pain and drama can be born.

It must also then be the cleric's I—the poet—who creates the final vision of the *Journal,* i.e., the vision of the mother sun, as protective, beautiful, and nurturing as the storm was destructive and ugly. Toward evening in the mountains, after the storm has subsided, the cleric sees a lamb with large, sad eyes, "a dumb eternal protest against the separation between souls" (229). The pathetic animal causes him to feel the inevitable alienation between one being and another; and as if in answer to his own protest, the sun vision is born. It is reminiscent of the prose poem "Roses," in which "roses and red and rose petals" fill the air. The evening sky is full of roses—light reds and deep reds—and right in the middle of them all, a single burning bud, the sun. It looks gently upon him "with a smile like a great mother's who in infinite, luxurious peace stands with her children at her ripe, heavy breasts . . ." (230). It is, it would seem, the beautiful moment of rebirth which Obstfelder sought to experience again and again. It was like the first morning, the cleric says; nothing was hurried, everything had time. He finally knows the peace of life. The sun falls slowly behind the horizon, and will continue to fall, and all the other suns, too, will glide in the "majestic sensuality of peace" (230).

Then the sun seems to speak to him of her superiority to the deadly, masculine god. She is greater, she says, than the dark thunder cloud, the wild, jagged rocks, and the sharp lightning. The cleric's spirit, she accuses, seeks the darkness, and his god force and destruction. She is neither dark nor sharp of form, but round and beautiful. The round shape, associated earlier with the disturbing restlessness and multiplicity of the modern world, becomes a symbol of nurture as she asserts the power of her beautiful image over the cleric's mental broodings, associated with the fatal god: ". . . you have lost yourself in abstractions, all your truths are abstractions and therefore dead,—all your gods" (231). What, she asks, are all your abstractions "in comparison to the woman who stands in the middle of the shining, fragrant sun and lets her milk flow into rose-red lips from her majestic breasts?" (232).

In the union of the rose, the woman, and the sun Obstfelder found the perfect symbol for the cleric's "lost home" where his soul might be reborn. The round shape of the flower, the mother's breast, and the sun is the powerful sign of both creation and eternity. Both the mother and the sun give life, but as rhythm brought peace to the principle of light in constant motion, the woman brings peace to the sun, as, indeed, the gentle heaving of the mother's breast brings calm to the child. The mother sun generates and perpetuates life, thus preserving the cleric's sense of self. She surrounds him, she does not penetrate him as the storm did; she lifts him upward, she does not throw him to the ground; she protects him, she does not harm him.

The cleric is, temporarily at least, renewed and made whole by the sun; and the *Journal* ends as he descends the mountain, heady with the fragrance of life.

And then I walked down from the glaciers toward human beings, as the fragrance grew, became fuller and fuller, pine, pine and birch, hazel and flower and brook, and finally all of it, everything, forest and oceans and roses and dew and mist and summer.(234)

There is, however, no reason to believe that the cleric's reconciliation with life will be lasting.[13] His vacillation in mood from one extreme to its opposite remains the *Journal*'s most powerful dynamic and its only constant. The stink of sin and fear will once again fill his nostrils, and the beautiful image of the mother sun will be darkened by the endless questions that torture this sad man who is guilty because he is alive. But although no permanent resolution is reached, it is fitting that the final vision is the very essence of Obstfelder's poetry, the visual, sensual image. "Seeing" is not seeing through or behind things, as the cleric so often thinks it is, but rather giving shape to things. Obstfelder saw most clearly through simple, uncluttered forms: bare trees against the snow, a woman's dark silhouette, a bloodied sun, or a peering eye. The most beautiful things, says the mother sun, are created in the image of me and your own earth. In other words, form is the key to vision.

Chapter Eight
Conclusion

In his poetry Sigbjørn Obstfelder sought above all else to give personal expression to his innermost feelings, particularly those feelings not yet consciously formulated and understood. As frightening as they could be and often were, they were his riches, a hidden spiritual treasure for which he had religious regard. They were himself in the ideal. In a sketch from the late 1880s he wrote, placing himself in a winter landscape:

> ——finally I have found a hallowed home where the most
> wonderful part of myself abides, spared, forgotten, something no
> one, no one knows, no one knows.
> . . . .
>   And if someone wants to come and rob me of it, he
> could not find it, because I have sunk it down into a deep,
> black lake which is iced over now, or in an unknown water-
> fall, . . . hidden [it] in a blueberry patch but it is now under the
> snow. And the other hiding places I won't reveal.
>   Those hiding places
>   and   the fine, flower-born moments.
> It is my discovery in the world, it is myself. No one can
> steal it without killing me. (III:109)

Of course, Obstfelder did reveal these hiding places through his poetry. They *became* his poetry, simply, and this in part explains why it is so filled with conflict, why it is such a mixture of guileless revelation and the persistent fear of exposure. He was entrapped, whether he chose to isolate himself in the peace of the black lake or to expose himself to the profane eyes of his readers. Both ways led to death but both were necessary for life.

The paradox informs everything Obstfelder wrote. His is a poetry longing for certainty, yet its conviction is doubt and its tendency is toward chaos. It is a poetry of psychological pain. The poet feels alone in a void, abandoned and fearing annihilation. Yet he would never exchange his isolation for the community's embrace. It is a poetry embued with a religious awe of life, yet it is profoundly nihilistic.

Such ambivalence was, of course, deeply rooted in the age, making Obstfelder one of its most relevant and disturbing spokesmen.

The quality of his work is uneven. Though he rewrote and rewrote, he was ultimately an experimenter, not a master, of forms, always searching for the one that would be the best and the most original medium. At times, particularly in the prose poems, he truly achieved that quality of expression for which all writers must strive; but at other times he was not so successful. His use of language was remarkable, simple in the extreme, capable of conveying both the halting utterances of a child in pain and the songs of a man in love, and singularly beautiful, as if tuned by the most sensitive ear. Yet its musicality could be achieved at the expense of profundity. And in truth, Obstfelder was not a thinker. He was a poet who "saw" things—himself, others, emotions, interactions, God—in physical shapes and primary colors. Strangely perhaps for a writer, he seemed more atuned to visual thinking, comprehending life in terms of concrete, often very sensual images. Thus a work like *A Cleric's Journal* is flawed because it goes against the grain of its author, whereas "The Belly" or "The Prisoner" or "I See" succeeds as it comes from the heart of his vision.

As it is difficult to determine the influence of specific writers on Obstfelder, it is difficult to determine his influence on specific writers after him. In terms of his experimentation with form and language, the emotional base of his poetry, and his haunted world view he is certainly the most significant precursor of Scandinavian Modernism. To greater and lesser degrees he can be said to have paved the way for, or directly influenced, or foreshadowed the works of the most prominent Scandinavian poets of the century, for example, in Sweden Pär Lagerkvist (1891–1974), Vilhelm Ekelund (1880–1949), Gunnar Ekelöf (1907–1968), Ragnar Jändel (1895–1939), and Tage Aurell (1895–1976); in Finland, Edith Södergran (1892–1923),

Rabbe Enckell (1903–1974), and Elmer Diktonius (1896–1961); and in Norway, Tarjei Vesaas (1897–1970) and Rolf Jacobsen (b. 1907).

Enckell (1903–1974), and Elmer Diktonius (1896–1961); and in Norway, Tarjei Vesaas (1897–1970) and Rolf Jacobsen (b. 1907).

In *Basar* (1978) Reidar Ekner recounted that he had once been speaking with Gunnar Ekelöf and had mentioned Obstfelder's poem "Spring." To Ekner's surprise Ekelöf's eyes lit up as he quoted, "To hell with castironpiles!" explaining that having read Obstfelder at an early age, he had felt an immediate kinship with the Norwegian's rebellious spirit. Obstfelder had obviously been a liberating force for the young Swedish poet, and Ekner wondered if Obstfelder may not possibly have "initiated more than *one* poetic revolution."[1] It is indeed possible and ultimately fitting that he who so longed to be free himself helped free the spirit of kindred Scandinavian poets.

Notes and References

Preface

1. All translations of Obstfelder's works as well as of Scandinavian secondary sources are my own unless otherwise indicated.

2. Sigbjørn Obstfelder, *Samlede skrifter*, 3 vols., ed. Solveig Tunold (Oslo, 1950). All references to works from *Samlede skrifter* are contained in the main body of the text.

Tunold's edition is the scholarly edition. Previous editions of Obstfelder's works are *Efterladte Arbeider. I Udvalg ved Viggo Stuckenberg.* (Copenhagen, 1903) and *Samlede skrifter*, 2 vols., ed. Carl Nærup (Oslo, 1917). Tunold's edition includes all of Nærup's *Samlede skrifter* and the works from *Efterladte Arbeider* which he did not include (with several minor exceptions) as well as yet unpublished works, as Tunold wrote, "on the basis of a thorough examination of all of the manuscript material at hand" (xii). Tunold also conscientiously did her best to correct the many errors, typographical and otherwise, that were to be found in the earlier editions.

3. This is not to say that there are not many fine, short works as yet unpublished. But much of the material is in draft form, and many of the pieces are variations of one or another work. Obstfelder was in the habit of endlessly rewriting, hoping finally to achieve perfection. The manuscripts in the archives are labeled Ms. 8, 165:a–e; Ms. 8, 1424:1–29; and Ms. 8, 1416.

Chapter One

1. Christian Claussen originally emphasized the motif of the eyes in two articles on Obstfelder from 1921, "Grundmotivet i Obstfelders digt-ning," *Tilskueren*, June 1921, pp. 412–21, and "Eiendomligheter i Obstfelders digtning," *Nordisk Tidsskrift*, 1921, pp. 514–27.

2. The Vigeland sketch for a statue that was never done appeared on the back cover of the literary journal *Basar* 1 (1978).

3. Hanna Pauli's *Vännerne* [The Friends, 1900–1907] hangs in the National Museum in Stockholm.

4. Hjalmar Söderberg, *Samlade verk* (Stockholm: Albert Bonnier, 1943), 9:160.

5. Gunnar Heiberg, "Obstfelder," *Ord och bild* 2 (1900):639.

6. Reidar Ekner, "Sigbjørn Obstfelder—En konturteckning," in his *En sällsam gemenskap* (Stockholm, 1967), p. 49. Ekner, Swedish poet and critic, has done one of the most serious and reliable studies on Obstfelder. Three essays, including the one cited above, plus "Obstfelders prosadikter," and "Obstfelders formproblem och formen i hans diktning," as well as a collection of six unpublished prose poems, appear in his book on Baudelaire, Söderberg, Obstfelder, and Rilke. The book is translated in the text as *A Strange Fellowship*.

7. Arne Hannevik, *Obstfelder og mystikken* (Oslo, 1960). Hannevik's study, written from the point of view of Obstfelder as a mystic, is by far the best and most complete critical work. In the present study Hannevik's book is relied upon as the most credible secondary source. A year prior to Hannevik's, another major book on the life and works of Obstfelder had been published, i.e., Johan Faltin Bjørnsen's *Sigbjørn Obstfelder* (Oslo, 1959). Hannevik pointed to any number of mistakes in the Bjørnsen book. See in particular Hannevik's long note, no. 13, pp. 274–76. Due to the unreliability of the Bjørnsen book, it has not been extensively used in this study. Hannevik's book is referred to in the text as *Obstfelder and Mysticism*.

8. Hannevik, p. 280.

9. Herman Obstfelder conveyed this information to the Norwegian psychiatrist Olav Kristian Brodwall, who reported it in his article "Sigbjørn Obstfelder. Digtning—personlighet og psykose," *Edda* 48 (1948): 362.

10. Letter to Ada Eckhoff, July 1, 1893, *Brev fra Sigbjørn Obstfelder,* ed. Arne Hannevik (Oslo, 1966), p. 82. All letters to persons other than Herman Obstfelder are included in this collection, which in further references will be referred to as *Brev*.

11. Up until 1814 Norway had been under Danish rule politically and, for all practical purposes, culturally. In 1814 Norway was ceded to Sweden. Although still under foreign rule until 1905, the country grew increasingly independent in its political, social, and cultural life.

12. Knut Hamsun, "Fra det ubevidste sjæleliv," *Samtiden* 1 (1890):325–44. The quotation is taken from an unpublished translation, "From the Unconscious Intellectual Life," trans. Marie Skramstad DeForest (Madison: University of Wisconsin, 1964).

13. Obstfelder's articles appeared in *Verdens Gang* on March 3, April 21, and May 5, 1894, and March 28, 1896.

14. Christoffer Brinchmann, *Dagbladet,* December 10, 1893.

15. Kristofer Randers, *Morgenbladet,* December 1893.

16. Hannevik, p. 22.

17. Hannevik, note 13, p. 275.

18. Edmund Wilson, *Axel's Castle* (New York and London: Charles Scribner's Sons, 1931; rpt. 1939), p. 21.

19. Letter to Olof Behrens and Eugenie Paulsen, January 6, 1892, *Brev*, p. 58.

20. Again, Herman Obstfelder conveyed this information to Dr. Brodwall, who reported it in his article in *Edda*, p. 360.

21. Letter to Herman Obstfelder, January 11, 1892, *Breve til hans bror*, ed. Solveig Tunold (Stavanger, 1949), p. 117. All letters to Herman Obstfelder are included in this collection.

22. Brodwall, p. 360.

23. The "Journal" begins on June 3, 1891, and ends with an entry addressed to "Hr. doktor!" written after Obstfelder had returned to Stavanger following his release from Frogner Colony. The "Journal" is included in the third volume of *Samlede skrifter*, pp. 131–70.

24. Letter to Jens Thiis, March 14, 1892, *Brev*, p. 60.

25. Letter to Dagny Bang, November 19, 1891, *Brev*, p. 56.

26. Critics have tended to accept Brodwall's diagnosis. Nevertheless, it can only be educated speculation since there was no patient to observe. Brodwall's exact opinion in Norwegian reads as follows: "Konklusjonen av disse overveielser blir, at en reaktiv schizofrent farget psykose antas som sannsynlighets-diagnose, mens muligheten for et ekte katatont Schub ikke kan utelukkes" (362).

27. Hannevik is the critic responsible for establishing the most correct picture of Obstfelder's comings and goings (see pp. 20–23).

28. Johan Faltin Bjørnsen reported that the hospital records recorded his illness as "Tuberc. pharyngis, laryngis og pulmonum" (266). Arne Hannevik, however, emphasized the fact that Obstfelder himself—again according to the hospital records—thought his illness had begun as a cold in December 1899 (note 36, p. 280).

Chapter Two

1. May 1890, *Breve til hans bror*, p. 77.

2. Elizabeth Sewell, *The Orphic Voice* (New Haven: Yale University Press, 1960), p. 325.

3. Referring to a personal conversation with Ekelöf, Reidar Ekner wrote: "Ekelöf told then that he had run across Obstfelder early, probably already in high school. He had also felt that way, rebellious. Obstfelder had felt liberating, like something of an order to march." *Basar* 1 (1978):18.

4. Rolf Nyboe Nettum, "Generasjonen fra 1890-årene," in *Norges litteraturhistorie* (Oslo, 1975), 4:118. Free verse was not, however, introduced into Norwegian poetry by Obstfelder. Nettum went on to say: "Rhymelessness was common in the lyrics of antiquity; it reappeared again during Romanticism—in Wergeland's poetry. Then it disappeared" (118).

5. Nettum, p. 119.

6. Ibid.

7. Charles Baudelaire, *Oeuvres complètes de Baudelaire, Petits poëmes en prose* (Paris: La Péiade, 1934), 2:4.

8. Hannevik, p. 14.

9. Ibid.

10. Ibid, p. 13.

11. Brodwall wrote of "Tempest" that it "does not speak of a genuine excess of vitality for life but it contains a violent ecstasy without emotional profundity" (386).

12. Octavio Paz, *The Bow and the Lyre* (*El Arco y la lira*, 1956), trans. Ruth L. C. Simms (Austin and London: University of Texas Press, 1973), p. 26.

13. Although during the spring of 1890 Obstfelder was writing enthusiastic letters to his sister and others about his hopes and plans, he was obviously having difficulty coping, his breakdown and inability to take the engineering exam being undeniable proof.

14. The poem takes its title from St. Paul's Epistle to the Romans, 8:22, which in the King James Version reads, "For we know that the whole creation groaneth and travaileth in pain together until now."

15. Arthur Edward Waite, *The Secret Tradition in Alchemy* (London and New York: Knopf, 1926), pp. 362–67. Obstfelder was not without knowledge of alchemical symbols, as can be seen in his plays, particularly *In Spring* and *The Red Drops*. See Chapter 6.

16. Ekner, *Gemenskap*, pp. 79–80.

17. Nettum, p. 117.

18. Baudelaire, in his poem "La Chambre double." "On the walls no artistic horrors: in relation to pure dream, unanalyzed impressions, the positive definition of art is blasphemy. Here, all is harmony of just sufficient light and delicious obscurity." Taken from *Poison and Vision*, ed. and trans. David Paul (New York: Vintage Books, 1974), p. 133.

19. Anna Balakian, *The Symbolist Movement: A Critical Appraisal* (New York: 1967), p. 100.

20. Interestingly he wrote a poem in English entitled "Til en 'Miss,'"

dated November 1890, Milwaukee (I:83–85). He also wrote "Fantasi" [Fantasy, I:25–26] dated December 1890. It was included in *Poems* and belongs to the early erotic poetry.

21. Found in Ms. 8, 1424:5.

Chapter Three

1. "Rhytmiske stemninger," *Samtiden* 3 (1892):254–56.

2. Letter to Jens Thiis, August 7, 1892, *Brev*, p. 65.

3. *Breve til hans bror*, p. 259.

4. Letter to Jens Thiis, November 10, 1892, *Brev*, p. 77.

5. Hannevik, p. 121.

6. Balakian, p. 10.

7. Johannes Jørgensen, "Charles Baudelaire," *Tilskueren*, September 1891, p. 707.

8. Letter to Ada Eckhoff, postmarked December 17, 1893, *Brev*, p. 85.

9. Balakian, p. 117.

10. Of the following four poems, three, "He Sows," "Yearning," and "Agony," are undated. Hannevik concluded that they were most likely written during this initial period (99–100).

11. In terms of Norwegian literature, Obstfelder learned a great deal, particularly stylistically speaking, from the folk ballad. See Ekner in *Gemenskap*, pp. 103–104.

12. Hannevik, p. 99.

13. Ibid., pp. 99–100.

14. See in particular the letters of May 7 and October 15, 1892, *Breve til hans bror*, pp. 132–38, 150–52.

15. Letter to Ellen Key, 1897, *Brev*, p. 188.

16. George Schoolfield, "Sigbjørn Obstfelder: A Study in Idealism," *Edda* 57 (1957):201.

17. Hannevik, p. 133.

18. The "good" translation was done in collaboration with Ross Shideler.

19. The Virgin Mary was a part of Obstfelder's fantasies during his breakdown. He referred to her specifically in the Frogner letter and in an unsent letter to an American friend, Dode Murphy (Ms. 8, 1424:13). See also Ekner, *Gemenskap*, specifically pp. 85–86.

20. Obstfelder was very taken by Walt Whitman, whose influence is unmistakable in this poem. In a letter to his brother postmarked December 8, 1892, he wrote: "I am working on some poems in the American Indian tone, a glorification of Pampas, in wild, colorful Indian images—and perhaps

they'll be an Ode to America—. . . . Yes, that idea has also occurred to me, go back to America, really learn English, become Whitman's, Foster's successor" (154).

21. Ekner, who has a very fine discussion of the mother goddess in *En sällsam gemenskap,* wrote that it was "conceivable that [Obstfelder]—unbeknown to himself—illustrates an archetypal idea" (83).

22. Balakian, p. 52.

23. Hannevik, p. 14.

24. The poem is undated. Hannevik felt it must have been written sometime after the trip to Paris due to its "rich, peaceful execution" (133).

25. Hannevik, p. 136.

26. C. G. Jung, "Psychologische Typen" (1921), excerpted in *C. G. Jung: Psychological Reflections,* ed. Jolande Jacobi (New York: Harper and Row, 1953; rpt. 1961), p. 100.

27. Jung, "Die psychologischen Aspekte des Mutterarchetypus" (1939), excerpted in *Psychological Reflections,* pp. 101–102.

28. Nettum, p. 29.

29. Hannevik, p. 113. Also his note 136, p. 286.

30. The "good" translation was done in collaboration with Ross Shideler.

31. Asbjørn Bergaas, "Sigbjørn Obstfelder: 'Jeg ser.'," *Samlaren* 33 (1952):12.

32. See his letter to his brother, March 14, 1892, p. 129. Also Brodwall, p. 361. Hannevik tended to view the "new" belief in God as a basic change. See particularly pp. 93–97. I personally have not been able to detect any lasting, *fundamental* alteration in Obstfelder's world view.

33. Letter undated but received on July 25, 1892, *Breve til hans bror,* p. 145.

Chapter Four

1. Part of the first section of this chapter on the prose poem and the analysis of the "The Belly" originally appeared—in a slightly different version—in my article, "Obstfelder's Prose Poem in General and in Particular," *Scandinavian Studies* 50 (1978):177–85.

2. Precisely what is and what is not a prose poem in Obstfelder's authorship is a matter of interpretation. He himself drew up two lists—which share many of the same poems—the first entitled "Små digte" [Little Poems] and designated as Ms. 8, 1424:2, and the second designated as Ms. 8, 1424:1. In *Samlede skrifter* Solveig Tunold chose not to publish all the poems on the combined lists—she published primarily according to the second

list (Ms. 8, 1424:1), calling it "S.b." (Siste bearbeidelse)—as prose poems but published some of them elsewhere in the section of *Samlede skrifter* entitled "Blandet prosa" [Mixed Prose], which is vol. III. Some she did not publish at all. Several prose pieces, including one from the second list (Ms. 8, 1424:1), "Det gamle hus" [The Old House], were published by Ekner as prose poems, first in *En sällsam gemenskap*, pp. 63–73, and later in *Basar* 1 (1978):18–23. See Ekner in *Gemenskap* for a publication of the lists, pp. 74–77.

3. Hannevik, p. 144. Hannevik's translation of Baudelaire is from *Oeuvres complètes de Baudelaire* (Paris: La Péiade, 1934),2:4.

4. Ekner, *Gemenskap*, p. 109. See pp. 99–109 for a good discussion of Obstfelder's style.

5. Edgar Allan Poe, "The Philosophy of Composition" (1846), *Great Short Works of Edgar Allan Poe*, ed. G. R. Thompson (New York: Harper & Row, 1970), p. 531.

6. James Kugel, *The Techniques of Strangeness in Symbolist Poetry* (New Haven and London, 1971), p. 38.

7. Ibid., pp. 43–73.

8. Ibid., p. 29.

9. Published first in *Gemenskap*, p. 63, and then in *Basar*, p. 18.

10. Letter to Ada Eckhoff, postmarked December 17, 1893, *Brev*, p. 85.

11. Letter to Ragna Dons, January 1894, *Brev*, p. 90.

12. Letter to Borghild Bjørklund, June 22, 1894 (?), *Brev*, p. 96.

13. Quoted from Brodwall, p. 367. This letter—dated November 18, 1891—was sealed until 1970 at the request of Herman Obstfelder. Brodwall, however, was allowed access to it when he wrote his article in 1948. Although the letter should now be available to the general public I was unable to see it, due, it would seem, to misguided protectiveness on the part of the librarians at Universitetsbibliotek, where the Obstfelder archives are kept. References to the letter are thus quoted from Brodwall.

14. Letter postmarked September 1893, *Breve til hans bror*, p. 172.

15. Brodwall, p. 371.

16. See note 18, Chapter 2.

17. Obstfelder's poem appeared in Johannes Jørgensen's *Taarnet*, February 1894, pp. 228–29. Vilhelm Krag had written a prose poem with the same title, "Nat," published in 1892. Obstfelder had been very moved by Krag's poem and wrote him a letter to that effect. The letter is published in *Samlede skrifter*, III:236–47. It is unknown whether the letter was ever sent.

18. Hannevik, p. 155.

19. See note 17.

20. Brodwall, p. 373.

21. Hannevik, p. 232.

22. Brodwall, p. 373.

23. Hannevik grouped these poems together (148). "The Worm" and "The Wasp" are undated; "Housewife" is from the fall of 1892; but Hannevik detected a similar tone, and, of course, the insect motif is common to all three. I have preserved Hannevik's grouping as it does nicely bring out the theme of finding the great in the small. There can, however, be no comparison—and Hannevik would agree—between the quality of the first two poems and the third.

24. The image of the butterfly occurred in the Frogner letter as a symbol of sexuality and fertility. See Brodwall, p. 369.

25. Gerhard Munthe's paintings were exhibited in the winter of 1893. See Hannevik, p. 150, and his note 170, p. 288.

26. Hannevik, p. 168.

27. On both of the lists of prose poems drawn up by Obstfelder "The Prisoner" is the first poem. It is also the first of the prose poems in *Samlede skrifter*. The poem is a fitting beginning for a collection of his prose poems or Obstfelder's work in general, conveying as it does the helplessness of the spirit.

Chapter Five

1. Hannevik, pp. 175–76.

2. The article was published in *Illustreret Tidende,* August 19, 1900.

3. Niels Ingwersen, "Den forsvundne episke forudsætning.Strejftog i 1890ernes nordiske prosa," in *Nordisk litteraturhistorie: en bog til Brøndsted* (Odense, 1979), pp. 285–86.

4. Ibid., p. 291.

5. Ibid., p. 287.

6. Apart from the initial reference to each story, all further references in the text will include only page numbers. "Liv," 'The Plain," and *The Cross* are included in vol. II of *Samlede skrifter.* "Autumn" and "The Unknown One" are included in vol. III.

7. Published first in *Nyt Tidsskrift* 2 (1894):553–64, and then together with "The Plain" as *To novelletter* (Bergen, 1895).

8. Susan Sontag, *Illness as Metaphor* (New York: Farrar, Straus and Giroux, 1978), p. 25.

9. Hannevik, p. 188.

10. Ibid., p. 164. "Autumn" was published in *Samtiden* 7 (1896):81–83.

11. Letter to Andreas Aubert, postmarked January 12, 1895, *Brev*, p. 108.

12. Published together with "Liv" as *To novelletter* (Bergen, 1895).

13. Letter to Ragna Dons, January-February 1895 (?), *Brev*, p. 110.

14. Hannevik, p. 175.

15. Ibid., pp. 164–65.

16. Originally published (Copenhagen, 1896). The text in *Samlede skrifter* is according to the 3rd ed. (Copenhagen, 1897).

17. Letter to Georg Brandes, August 1896, *Brev*, p. 150.

18. Ibid., p. 151.

19. Hannevik, p. 186.

20. Published in *Verdens Gang*, August 17, 1895.

Chapter Six

1. Letter to Christofer Brinchmann, August 1896, *Brev*, p. 149.

2. Hannevik suggested that Obstfelder never really successfully finished the play but finally allowed it to be published. He was, Hannevik pointed out, in economic need at the time (103). The play was published in *Samtiden* 10 (1899):129–40.

3. He based the dating on the similarity of theme in this play and in "The Plain" and *The Cross* (193).

4. Published (Copenhagen, 1897). According to Hannevik the book was given "a rather unfriendly reception by the critics" (212). He noted too that the play was possibly performed in Copenhagen in February 1898 (212) with disastrous results if it were indeed put on (note 219, p. 290).

5. Maurice Maeterlinck, "The Tragical in Daily Life," in *The Treasure of the Humble (Le Trésor des humbles,* 1896), trans. Alfred Sutro (New York: Dodd, Mead and Co., 1900), p. 98.

6. Maeterlinck, "The Tragical in Daily Life," pp. 105–106.

7. Letter to Johanne Dybwad, Autumn 1896, *Brev*, p. 157. The critical portion of this letter is also published in *Samlede skrifter*, I:184–88.

8. Apart from the initial reference to each play, all further references in the text will include only page numbers. All the plays are included in vol. I of *Samlede skrifter.*

9. There is a marked similarity between the man's attraction to Esther and the poet's attraction to the death goddess in the poem "Ene" [Alone, I:10–13]. Obstfelder was working on them both in 1892.

10. Jung, "Individual Dream Symbolism in Relation to Alchemy," a translation, with minor alterations made at the insistence of the author, of *Psychologie und Alchemie* (Zurich, 1944; 2nd ed., revised, 1952), part II of vol. 12 of the *Collected Works,* and included in *The Portable Jung,* ed. Joseph Campbell (New York: Penguin, 1971; rpt. 1977), p. 355.

11. Letter to Johanne Dybwad, autumn 1896, *Brev,* p. 159.

12. Ibid., p. 157.

13. Ibid.

14. Ibid., p. 158.

15. Hannevik, p. 224.

16. Hannevik pointed out that in his last years Obstfelder became more interested in the political life of the time, for example, the Dreyfus case. Hannevik saw *The Last King* as Obstfelder's greatest effort toward a more politically relevant literature (226–28). Nevertheless, from the first act it seems that Obstfelder would have had difficulty writing a socially engagé drama.

Chapter Seven

1. Aside from the first reference, all references in the text will include only page numbers. The *Journal* is included in vol. II of *Samlede skrifter.*

2. Postmarked September 1893, *Breve til hans bror,* p. 169.

3. Letter to Signe Hansen, July 1897 (?), *Brev,* p. 185.

4. Postmarked September 1893, *Breve til hans bror,* p. 172.

5. Letter to Ellen Key, May 1900, *Brev,* p. 228.

6. Published (Copenhagen, 1900). His widow and publisher published the manuscript immediately upon his death. There were any number of errors in the first edition which were carried over into later ones. They were corrected in *Samlede skrifter.* See editor's note, II:291–92.

7. In *The Temper of Norwegian Literature* James McFarlane wrote, for example, "It is a book with the courage of its lack of convictions" (New York and Toronto, 1960), p. 111.

8. See Chapter 3, note 32.

9. Letter to Ellen Key, May 1900, *Brev,* p. 228.

10. Letter to Wilhelm Andreas Wexelsen, spring 1898, *Brev,* p. 200.

11. *Breve til hans bror,* p. 268.

12. See Schoolfield, *Edda* 57 (1957):193–223, for an excellent discussion of particularly this section of the *Journal.*

13. This interpretation is based on internal textual evidence. Hannevik would, I think, agree. Regarding some unpublished drafts of a continuation

of the *Journal* (Ms. 8, 1424:26) in which the cleric sustains an even more ecstatic state than in the final scene in the published version, Hannevik wrote, "... there is reason to believe that also the unpublished continuation only depicts a new *stage* in his mind's restless oscillation between different religious beliefs" (262).

Chapter Eight

1. Ekner, *Basar,* p. 18.

Selected Bibliography

PRIMARY SOURCES

1. Works in Norwegian

Brev fra Sigbjørn Obstfelder. Edited with an introduction by Arne Hannevik. Oslo: Gyldendal, 1966.

Breve til hans bror. Edited with an introduction by Solveig Tunold. Stavanger: Stabenfeldt, 1949.

De røde dråber. Copenhagen: Gyldendalske Forlag, 1897.

Digte. Bergen: Grieg, 1893.

Efterladte Arbeider. I Udvalg ved Viggo Stuckenberg. With a postscript. Copenhagen: Gyldendalske Forlag, 1903.

En prests dagbog. Copenhagen: Gyldendalske Boghandel, 1900.

Esther. Samtiden 10 (1899):129–40.

Korset. Copenhagen: Gyldendalske Forlag, 1896.

Samlede skrifter. 2 vols. Edited with an introduction by Carl Nærup. Oslo: Gyldendal, 1917.

Samlede skrifter. 3 vols. Edited with an introduction by Solveig Tunold. Oslo: Gyldendal, 1950.

"Seks prosastykker og et dikt." Edited by Reidar Ekner. *Basar* 1 (1978):18–23. The prose pieces were previously published in *En sällsam gemenskap* (1967).

To novelletter. Bergen: Greig, 1895.

2. Works in English

"Nocturne," "I Look" (here translated as "I See"), "The Rose," "Torture" (here translated as "Agony"), and "Barcarole" in *Anthology of Norwegian Lyrics*. Translated by Charles Wharton Stork. Princeton: Princeton University Press, 1942.

Poems from the Norwegian of Sigbjørn Obstfelder. Translated by P. Selver. Oxford: The Vincent Works, 1920.

SECONDARY SOURCES

1. Relating specifically to Obstfelder.
Aal, Anathon, "Sigbjørn Obstfelder." *Samtiden* 11 (1900):298-303. Rather emotional and idealistic portrait of Obstfelder by his childhood friend. Articles of this nature contributed to the Obstfelder myth.
Anonymous. Review of *Poems from the Norwegian of Sigbjørn Obstfelder.* Translated by P. Selver. *Times Literary Supplement,* November 7, 1920, p. 730. Enthusiastic review not so much of Selver but of Obstfelder.
Aurell, Tage. "Sigbjørn Obstfelder—En studie." *Ord och bild* 31 (1922):217-26.
Bergaas, Asbjørn. "Sigbjørn Obstfelder: 'Jeg ser.' "*Samlaren* 33 (1952):11-19. A fine close reading of "I See."
Beyer, Edvard. "Arne Hannevik: Obstfelder og mystikken." *Edda* 62 (1962):112-32. Criticism of Hannevik's doctoral thesis which was *Obstfelder og mystikken.*
Beyer, Harald. "The Lyric Renaissance." In *A History of Norwegian Literature.* Translated by Einar Haugen. New York: New York University Press, 1956, pp. 258-64. Short introduction in English to Obstfelder, Krag, and Vogt.
Bjørnsen, Johan Faltin. *Sigbjørn Obstfelder.* Oslo: Gyldendal, 1959. Deals with life and works. Much interesting material but not always accurate.
Brodwall, Olav Kristian. "Sigbjørn Obstfelder." Diktning—personlighet og psykose." *Edda* 48 (1948):353-90. Psychoanalytic analysis of Obstfelder's mental breakdown and its traces in his works.
Brøgger, Niels Chr. "Sigbjørn Obstfelder." In *Norsk biografisk leksikon.* Oslo: Aschehoug, 1949, X:305-14. General introduction to Obstfelder's works. Stresses particuarly the theme of angst.
Claussen, Christian. "Eiendomligheter i Obstfelders digtning."*Nordisk Tidsskrift* (1921), pp. 514-27. Study of themes in Obstfelder's work.
———. "Grundmotivet i Obstfelder digtning." *Tilskueren,* June 1921, pp. 412-21. Study of themes.
Ekelund, Vilhelm. *Antikt ideal.* Malmö: Aktiebolget Framtiden, 1909, pp. 71-76 and 80 and following.
Ekner, Reidar. "Obstfelder." *Basar* 1 (1978):16-18. Introduction to Obstfelder, in particular as a forerunner of Modernism, and to the prose pieces published in the same issue.
———. "Sigbjørn Obstfelder—en konturteckning." "Sex efterlämnade prosastycken." "Obstfelders prosadikter." "Obstfelders formproblem

och formen i hans diktning." In En sällsam gemenskap. Stockholm: Norstedt, 1967. Six as yet unpublished prose pieces (later published in *Basar*) and three fine essays on Obstfelder in a cultural/historical context, and themes and forms in his work.

Haakonsen, Daniel. "Arne Hannevik: Obstfelder og mystikken." *Edda* 62 (1962):89-111. Criticism of Hannevik's doctoral thesis.

Hannevik, Arne. *Obstfelder og mystikken*. Oslo: Gyldendal, 1960. The major work on Obstfelder.

————. "Obstfelders 'Jeg ser' analysert à la Cleanth Brooks." *Samlaren* 33 (1952):36-43. Excellent close reading of "I See."

Heiberg, Gunnar. "Obstfelder." *Ord och bild* 2 (1900):636-40. A translation into Swedish of Heiberg's fine, personal remembrance of Obstfelder as a personality and a poet. Originally appeared in *Verdens Gang* August 18, 1900.

Ingwersen, Niels. "Den forsvunde episke forudsætning. Strejftog i 1890ernes nordiske prosa." In *Nordisk litteraturhistorie—en bog til Brønsted*. Odense: Universistetsforlag, 1979, pp. 277-96. Excellent study of the prose of the 1890s. Obstfelder is one of Ingwersen's models.

Krag, Vilhelm. *Dengang vi var tyve aar*. Oslo: Aschehoug, 1927. Krag's remembrances of his time and his artist friends. Contains several interesting anecdotes about Obstfelder.

McFarlane, James. "Sigbjørn Obstfelder." In *The Temper of Norwegian Literature*. London: Oxford University Press, 1960, pp. 104-13. Very insightful sketch of Obstfelder as a writer in the context of his time.

Nag, Martin. "Var Obstfelder redd eller modig?" *Samtiden* 62 (1953):534-40. Primarily an analysis of "I See."

Nettum, Rolf N. "Generasjonen fra 1890-årene." In *Norges litteraturhistorie*. Oslo: Cappelen, 1975, IV:8-29, 110-27. Excellent analysis of the age in general and of Obstfelder's works specifically.

Nilsson, Josef, "Sigbjørn Obstfelders mystik." *Edda* 33 (1933):344-68. Good study of Obstfelder's mystical strain. Particularly interesting analysis of the women in his works.

Norseng, Mary Kay. "Obstfelder's Prose Poem in General and in Particular." *Scandinavian Studies* 50 (1978): 177-85. Primarily a study of Obstfelder's literary techniques in the prose poem.

Rode, Helge. "Det sjælelige gennembrud." In *Det sjælelige gennembrud. Udvalgte Kritiker. II*. Copenhagen: Gyldendalske Boghandel, 1928, pp. 14-46. Rode's lecture—originally given in 1913—analyzing the spirit of the 1890s is an interesting contemporary view of the times and provides a good context in which to view Obstfelder.

Sandemose, Axel. "Møte med Arne Dybfest og Sigbjørn Obstfelder." In *Rejsen til Kjørkelvik.* Copenhagen: Reitzel, 1954. Actually mostly about Axel Sandemose.

Schoolfield, George. "Sigbjørn Obstfelder: A Study in Idealism." *Edda* 57 (1957):193–223. Very interesting study of Obstfelder's works, particularly of *A Cleric's Journal.*

Thiis, Jens, "Nittiårene og 'Samtiden.'" *Samtiden* 49 (1940):26–31. As remembered by Thiis, an interesting portrait of the times, his friend, Obstfelder, and the beginning of New Romanticism.

Winsnes, A. H. "Sigbjørn Obstfelder." In *Norges litteratur.* Oslo: Aschehoug, 1961, V:243–54. This is the principal Norwegian literary history. It gives a general introduction to Obstfelder.

Øyselebø, Olaf. "Obstfelders bruk av apposisjonssyntaks." In *Dikteren—og språkets muligheter.* Oslo: Universitetsforlag, 1976, pp. 73–102. Study of Obstfelder's syntax, using *A Cleric's Journal.*

2. Relating to the Symbolist Movement

Balakian, Anna. *The Symbolist Movement: A Critical Appraisal.* New York: Random House, 1967. Excellent general discussion and evaluation of the movement.

Kugel, James. *The Techniques of Strangeness in Symbolist Poetry.* New Haven and London: Yale University Press, 1971. Fine discussion of Symbolist techniques.

Wilson, Edmund. *Axel's Castle.* New York and London: Charles Scribner's Sons, 1931; rpt. 1939. The classic.

Index